Saul Rubinek is best known as an actor. He has been seen in such films as *Sweet Liberty*, *Wall Street* and *Against All Odds*. He won a Genie Award for Best Supporting Actor in Ralph Thomas's *Ticket to Heaven* and earned nominations for his roles in Claude Jutra's *By Design* and in *The Outside Chance of Maximillian Glick*.

Saul Rubinek was born in a Displaced Persons camp in Germany in 1948 and came to Canada with his parents in 1949. He worked as a child actor in stage and radio and became a member of Stratford Company at 20. He was a founding member of the Toronto Free Theatre and has worked extensively on Canadian stages and on the CBC. Saul Rubinek divides his time between Toronto and New York (and Los Angeles if he has to).

1980 edm.

So Many Miracles

— by —

Saul Rubinek

Penguin Books

PENGUIN BOOKS
Published by the Penguin Group
Penguin Books Canada Ltd, 2801 John Street, Markham, Ontario L3R 1B4
Penguin Books Ltd, 27 Wrights Lane, London W8 5TZ, England
Viking Penguin Inc., 40 West 23rd Street, New York, New York 10010, USA
Penguin Books Australia Ltd, Ringwood, Victoria, Australia
Penguin Books (NZ) Ltd, 182-190 Wairau Road, Auckland 10, New Zealand

Penguin Books Ltd, Registered Offices: Harmondsworth, Middlesex, England

First published in Viking by Penguin Books Canada Limited, 1988

Published in Penguin Books, 1989

1 3 5 7 9 10 8 6 4 2

Manufactured in Canada

Canadian Cataloguing in Publication Data
Rubinek, Saul.
So many miracles

ISBN 0-14-010381-3

I. Title.

PS8585.U26S6 1989   C813'.54   C87-094862-8
PR9199.3.R824S6   1989

British Library Cataloguing in Publication Data Available
American Library of Congress Cataloguing in Publication Data Available

There are so many miracles, but I dedicate this book to one of them, the most ordinary miracle, the one that remains a daily wonder: the love my mother and father found, kept, and shared.

ACKNOWLEDGEMENTS

Kate Lynch lived with me throughout the writing of this book and was the first one who believed that my parents' voices on tape could be heard on the page. Kate kept me going.

The Canada Council had an Explorations Grant program in 1977 for artists who had established themselves in one field and wanted to explore another. I was hardly established as an actor at that time, and for whatever rules were bent, and for the Council's enlightened decision to give me some money so that I could afford to even begin to write this, my thanks.

My thanks to Susan Mander and Cathy Lineham, not only for transcribing the material but for their involvement with the work, their emotional dedication. I'd like to thank Lorraine Johnson at Penguin for putting up with me at my fussiest.

My friends were the first to read this and tell me that, yes, you don't have to necessarily be a friend, or Jewish, to get more than a little something from this book. Without friends, no guts.

Thank you Pam Bernstein, Eric Bick, Maury Chaykin, Matt Craven, Shain Jaffe, Claude Jutra, Vivienne Leebosh, Nick Mancuso, Brian Riordan, Barbara Smith, Marilyn Szatmary, Ralph Thomas, Barbara Williams, Ralph Zimmerman.

To Cynthia Good, my editor, who believed, fought and bought, my eternal gratitude.

Introduction

This book began as a kind of subterfuge. I am my parents' only child. Ten years ago, I fell in love with a girl and we started living together. She wasn't Jewish. My father said Kaddish, the prayer for the dead. My mother was caught in the middle, not wanting to go against her husband, not wanting me out of their lives. To tell the truth, I never really took the Kaddish thing all that seriously. First of all, my father said the prayer for the dead for *himself*, not for me. If you think about it, that didn't really cut me off, it just told me, in no uncertain terms, what I'd done to him. I also knew my mother would work on him.

However, we weren't on speaking terms, my father and I. My mother and I spoke — a language of recrimination and tears. Something had to be done, so after six months I invented this book. I figured I'd tell my mother I was planning to write about their experiences in Poland, before, during and after the war. I was coming to see her with tape recorder in hand. If Dad didn't want to talk to me, fine. But I knew he wouldn't be able to stay out of it. He'd hear my mother tell a few stories that didn't happen quite the way he remembered them, and that would be that: we'd be talking — formally, through a tape recorder, but talking. I had no intention of writing a book — I lied. It was a way back to my parents without direct confrontation.

It turned out the way I thought it would — with a few differences. The formality of interviews on tape forced me to see my parents in a new light. When I was a boy, I thought everyone's mother and father had nightmares, cried in the night. I grew up with their stories, but they didn't actually sit down and tell them to me — I overheard them: they would remind each other or argue about certain incidents; they would share experiences with friends who had also gone through it. And these stories were repeated, over and over, until they became part of my imagination as surely as it was part of their history. The stories I remembered from my youth — painted in black and white — slowly lost the quality of nightmare tales from the Holocaust. I began to understand my parents as individual human beings, I could identify with them, and for the first time, their history became something I could cope with, valuable for my own life.

I thought that buried somewhere in my father's life I would find a reason for his violent reaction to my Catholic girlfriend. Many times I felt I grasped it, and then it would slip away from me, too easy an answer, not acceptable. In any case, quite apart from my attempts to manipulate events, my mother and father came to accept the woman I loved.

I was twenty-eight when I started the interviews. I'm writing this introduction ten years later. The years have allowed me time to think about what questions to ask my parents. And time taught me to understand why I'm writing this book for others to read. My parents' reaction to this book has been — "Everybody knows about the war. Who needs more stories about it?" But this isn't about the war. It's about them.

Part One

If you didn't know any better, this was a good life. But I think I knew better. I had a very good life, a nice family, in our little town of Pinczow but if I lived in a big city, it would be better. I always liked a big city. I went almost every winter to my grandfather's place in Lublin because I wanted to have a good time and I wanted to visit my grandparents, so my parents let me go. My grandmother didn't know what to do for me first. I remember once I didn't want to go back to Pinczow. Well, in Lublin I used to go out with boys. And uncle Leon took me everywhere. He lived together with my grandparents in Lublin. My grandmother died just before the war, in '38 or '37 — cancer she had — but she was still alive when I was coming there. I remember as a young girl, Leon took me to night-clubs, and I had a ball. It was a novelty for me, you know. In fact, he wanted to marry me. Leon was dying to marry me but I didn't want him because I saw that he didn't have a good character. I didn't go for that.

Leon was my father's brother but only five years older than me. An uncle you could marry — you cannot marry an aunt in Jewish law, but an uncle is okay.

My grandmother used to say to me, "Why don't you want Leon? He's such a nice boy..." After all, he was going to Warsaw to buy everything for the business for my grandfather. "...a very able boy. Why don't you want him?"

So I didn't want to say he hasn't got a good character. My grandmother didn't know that, but I knew.

Before the war, you needed a dowry. And there was Sarah, Leon's sister. She was very short, she didn't have a good figure, she wasn't so pretty, I would say. But a good soul; the best. And Leon was the businessman. I knew that he saved up ten thousand zlotys — like today ten thousand dollars — in a bank account, for himself, he should have some money on his own. And he knew he's got a sister, and that my grandfather didn't have any cash. It's not like here, you have money in the bank, or you have bonds or certificates, investments. In Poland, it wasn't like that: you had a nice living, a beautiful home, with meals regular, decent. But no cash. So he knew that my grandfather didn't have any money, and he's got a sister, Sarah, who wasn't so pretty, and my grandfather needs some money to marry her off. And Leon could save money on the side, from my grandfather's business? I didn't like that. So I didn't want to marry him.

I was the oldest girl. If you're the oldest, you have everything. Because at home you had to wait your turn. There wasn't such a thing that the younger one will marry before and the older later. Everything was in line, by age. I remember, we laughed so much, when they were matchmaking for me, so many different matches, and I didn't want to hear about it because I was in love with Israel, so my little sister Malkale, she was just a young kid, she used to say, "I'm not going to wait for you! If you're not going to get married, I'm not going to wait for you!" We laughed so much.

In our little town of Pinczow I couldn't go out with anybody. What are you talking, to go out with a boy? Religious people, like my parents were? Never. That was today like, I don't know, you go and convert.

I knew Israel since 1936. I was just a child, sixteen years old. I met him at a wedding, I remember. My uncle's wife died, so he remarried and it happened she was a friend of Israel's aunt. The bride's name was Tchaikowska, lovely girl, never before married, so she married this uncle of mine, the widower. The wedding was in the summertime, so it just happened Israel came to Pinczow. He always came for two months to his grandparents in the summertime because he didn't have work in that season in Lodz.

I remember I fell in love first. He didn't even know, the poor thing. There was an orchestra, Benzion Klezmer, ha! That was some orchestra, he couldn't even play, but he played anyway, on a fiddle, with his two helpers there. Mostly Chassidic people were dancing separate, not girls with boys. But Israel was dancing so beautiful with other girls, I was so jealous I could bust. Anyway, what could I do, I was so heartbroken, nobody asked me to dance, so I went home.

Well, what happened later? My brother Chamel wanted to know everything, so he wanted to know to dance too, even though he looked like the other Chassidic boys. He was very intelligent. You know that they kept him in concentration camp to the last minute? He had typhus and they cured him because they needed him in the office.

So he wanted to know how to dance and he figured he'll ask Israel for a few lessons. Well, Chamel and also my uncle Meyer spoke to Israel. But they had to have a room where to learn because this was outrageous, this was a shame to the family, to dance. They had to hide. There was a Jew in Pinczow, he already lived a little on the outskirts, an old Jew, but you could talk to him, he was a smart cookie. Mr Roit was his name. They knew that he has a whole house there, and upstairs lots of room.

"Mr Roit, we want to learn to dance, keep it quiet, and don't tell anything."

With him you could do anything, he said all right, nobody will know. My parents didn't know, God forbid. When Israel taught them a few steps, so a boy with a boy, how does it look to dance? Israel said why don't they bring their sisters, and they'll learn with a girl to dance. You know my mother had a younger sister, she was beautiful, you never seen such a beauty. My aunt Genya. She was only four years older than me. My grandmother got pregnant and then four years later, my mother was pregnant with me. Anyway, Israel said, "Bring your sisters and then you'll learn at least how to hold a girl."

My brother and my uncle came home and they talked to me and to my aunt Genya, we should come. I was so happy, because I was already in love with Israel. But how could I walk over to him and say I'm in love with you? And it's funny, I said to myself, that's going to be my husband, when I saw him the first time. He didn't know nothing. We started to dance and then Israel started to fall in love. We danced all the time. They said, "We brought her to be our partner, and she always dances with you!"

So that's when it started. And that's why my parents later said my brother is to blame.

My parents didn't want me to marry him. It was going on a war, it was terrible. Because he was an actor. With an actor, it's just like to marry, let's say, a bishop. And I have to say I was a very beautiful girl. Everything was by matchmakers, at that time. Your parents had to pay dowry, but for me they wanted to pay my parents. But I was in love with Israel. They knew that he's not religious, but they didn't care about that so much, they were very modest people, my parents. But they saw his picture on the front page of a magazine, they found out he was an actor, and that killed everything. He wasn't even allowed to come into the house. I met him all the time outside.

And another thing: "He's short. What's the matter with you? He's so short, what's the matter with you, you're such a beautiful girl."

I said, "I don't care he's short. He has a good heart. That's what I'm looking for in a husband."

I saw handsomer men, but I saw he had such a heart of gold, and that was why I fell in love, that's all.

Life was very nice, I went out with girlfriends. Only when Israel came every summer, naturally we walked together, such beautiful places. First of all — you know the corn how it's growing? — that was the country of corn. And mountains, the nicest mountains. I always used to say to Israel, if the mountains could talk, oh they would tell us stories. They had there mountain springs, and they used to say at home that if you drink this water, it could make you well.

In fact, I remember that my little brother Yossele was once sick, he had that special cough, a whooping cough. Maybe now they have a cure, but at that time not. When the spasm came, he started to cough. Usually as a child you get it, but he wasn't a child any more so the doctor didn't believe it. He asked him to come to the office and sit there till he's going to get this attack, to make sure that it's that cough and not something else. Good enough, it was that cough. It was terrible when the spasm came, it was awful. So they used to say, if you drink the water which is brought from the mountains — it was ice cold, and so clear, you just can't imagine how tasty this water was — if you go there before the sun comes up, and you take this water and you drink it, you're cured. So you think that my two older brothers didn't get up at four o'clock in the morning, Chamel and Srulcie? And they went. And it was far to go, to be there before the sun comes out. I don't even remember if it helped or not. I just remember the story of it, that they brought back that lovely water.

It was a nice life there. The only thing is that I couldn't live my way that I wanted to live, to be free more, to go out with somebody. I only could go out with girlfriends. One of my closest girlfriends was Tsivia Finestat, her father had a big textile business and believe me, she could have whatever clothes she wanted, but everything she had was filthy and she was always borrowing my skirts. She sold her soul because of her father. For a man to have a religious son-in-law who was sitting all day studying the Torah was considered the biggest honour. But who could afford to support him: only a rich father-in-law. Tsivia married a man like that for her father, not for herself. She wasn't even the type, she was such a modern girl, what did she want to prove? That she was a good daughter? Well, I told her she was a hypocrite but she married a man she didn't love and he used to sit all day learning and she became a religious wife, it didn't suit her a bit.

I liked better another friend because at least she was honest. Channah Zucker. She was double my age, a little bit on the fat side but a beautiful face and she was wearing make-up, gorgeous. My mother couldn't take it that I had a friend like this, so much older and not religious. But Channah was smart. Was she clever! That's what I liked about her. And such a smart dresser.

I have only one girlfriend from those days who lived through the war — Lola. She came from a family where the father was a horse-and-wagon driver but the children were all brought up in a lovely way because the mother was such a fine, quiet person. She was a beautiful girl, Lola. She lives now in Israel, in 1966 she came to visit me here in Ottawa for six months. Anyway, in Pinczow she belonged to Hashomer Hatsayir, a Zionist organization, and she took me once there. Oh, I liked it. A lot of boys, you know. But don't ask, when my parents found this out, I had to stop it right away. I would never do something to hurt my parents. Never. My father said this was not the place for me and I understood right away, that's it. From a religious home a girl should go out there with boys to entertain herself? From a religious home? You know that I was the first one in my family to fall in love, in the whole family? What do you mean, fall in love? That is a crime, like today, I don't even know how to name it.

Lola stayed in Hashomer Hatsayir, and there she met a boy, Zev, who fell in love with her. Zev went to Israel before the war but he promised to come back to Pinczow to marry Lola and take her back to Israel. And he did it.

It all brings back to me sad memories. You see, I had a friend, Goldie Kalb, who also was a friend to Lola and also belonged to Hashomer Hatsayir. She was the type I liked; she wanted to tell you something, she said it right away, no monkey-business. A very open girl, she had an exotic look about her. Goldie also fell in love with a boy from that Zionist group and just like with Lola and Zev, that boy went to Israel with a promise to come later and take her away. Well, Goldie watched when Zev came back for Lola and she was waiting for her boyfriend, she was so lost in love. She found out he married another girl in Israel and he never came back.

So Lola lived. Tsivia Finestat, Channah Zucker, and Goldie Kalb all went with the deportation to the camps and died.

I was never so religious. I believed in God but I was never religious. My father was very orthodox, but he didn't have the sidecurls. He had a beard, and he of course didn't go out without a hat, but he was not fanatical. Very religious, but normal.

I never did anything to hurt my parents but sometimes I did things that my parents didn't see. You know at home, on Saturdays a Gentile woman came in to make fire. A Jew must not work on the Sabbath. So what happened? You have to eat something warm. Well, before you put a match into the oven, all the food you're going to eat has to be ready on that oven on Saturday and then this Gentile woman came in. She was a widow, she didn't have anybody in Pinczow, and on the same yard where we had our house, she had a room there too. So she came in Saturday morning seven o'clock, made a fire and then later by twelve o'clock she came again and added some coals there because after all, the fire would go out. In Europe, it was like this in the religious homes. The parents on Saturdays came home from the synagogue, we had a big dinner and after that the parents go to sleep, in the afternoon. That was the style. So my friends and I were playing in the kitchen. And I was anaemic, even now I am, in blood. I'm always cold. I saw the fire is already going out there in that stove, so I made all my friends go to the other room and I closed the door, I should be left by myself in the kitchen. And then, fast, I took some coals and put in fast in the oven, the fire shouldn't go out, I should be warmer, because the Gentile woman didn't come back any more in the afternoon. My friends didn't know, that's why I made them go into the other room. I'll never forget it, when my mother got up from sleep, it was still warm there from this oven, the coals still red. She said, "The woman did it very well today, the heat lasts so long." I laughed so much to myself, I knew I threw the coals in the oven. And nobody saw. I would never say to anybody nothing, never. Not even my sisters.

We loved each other very much, the family. One for the other would give their head. Srulcie was the oldest of us children, next was Chamel, then there was one brother who died as a baby — I don't remember how — then came me, and that's why there were so many years between me and Chamel, because of that child between who died. Younger than me was Shaindele, then Yossele and Malkale was the youngest. So in 1936 Srulcie was twenty-six and Chamel twenty-four. I was sixteen, Shaindale fourteen, Yossele eleven, and Malkale nine.

An ordinary day, I got up in the morning, I never was an early riser. We had a very good breakfast, the baker was next door to us, fresh rolls, coffee, cocoa, eggs, butter, everything on the table that you wanted, on a yellow tablecloth. I'll never forget it, that tablecloth.

I slept with my sister Shaindele together in one bed because the house wasn't big enough, we didn't have too many rooms. What do you think, everybody had a separate bed to sleep? We always had a maid, a Jewish girl, she slept in the kitchen. You know that we had a maid when I was still a child, that came to us when she was only twelve or thirteen years old, and she was with us till she was twenty-five. She was one of the family.

Our house was on a square, in the middle was a garden, and all around sidewalks. From every corner of the square were streets leading off. For example, one street they called Busko Street because with this road you could go to the town of Busko Zdroj, where Israel's grandfather was a rabbi. And how many cars were there altogether, nobody had a car, but sometimes the bus went by that took people to Kielce, forty kilometres away, or a taxi.

Nobody had water in the house, you had to go to the garden

in the square and open a tap where the water was coming out. There used to be water-carriers, men who carried pails of water to deliver to the houses, and everybody had a barrel at home. But whatever he delivered, we were always short, because we were six children, and the maid makes seven, and my parents too, so we used a lot of water to wash ourselves and clothes, and the water-carrier couldn't bring so much. We always had two pails and we brought it ourselves, because how far was it? Just across the street, there was the garden, and there was this tap for everybody. I'll never forget, my father — you never seen such a good soul in your life — when he came from the flour mill and saw Esther, the maid, is walking with two pails of water, he ran right away and grabbed the two pails of water. She was a maid to us, and he didn't let her carry the pails of water. You understand what kind of person he was?

Esther left when Yossele was probably only two years old. I remember it, like in my dream, that all her family lived in Pinczow. She had a brother, he was always walking around wearing a white coat, like a raincoat. The whole town knew he was a Communist. He was, Israel told me he was. Esther's parents were very poor people, imagine if they gave a child away to another family to be a maid. I remember when Esther left us for Argentina where she had a brother, she left from our house, so all her family and everybody came to our place. It was summertime, they were sitting outside in the yard on chairs, to say goodbye to her. She was like one of the family, she cared so much, with all her heart. When she left, the kettle was boiling, I'll never forget this: imagine a young girl, twenty-five, going to Argentina from a small town like Pinczow, but she cared so much about the whole house, and the family, and my parents, that the kettle was boiling, and she was already walking out — I remember like now, in a hat and a blue coat — she went back, took some cold water and she added to the kettle. You see how she was? Very nice. I looked for her later, I wanted so much to find her but nobody was left from her family.

Anyway, nine o'clock in the morning we were all up, we had breakfast and then we had to open the store. We had a shoe store, and my parents had licence for schnapps to sell but we weren't allowed to give it out in glasses, only by bottle. We had wines too, but that didn't sell so well. The store was built together with the house, so when you walked into the house from the store, there were two doors with glass windows, we had curtains naturally, and the first room was my parents' bedroom. We didn't even have a living-room, that bedroom was a combination. Then was a dining-room, and after the dining-room was the kitchen, a big one. That's all we had. A whole week the store wasn't too busy, except Tuesdays and Fridays were market days, so all the farmers came into town and that's when we sold a lot of shoes.

At one o'clock every single day the table was set with a white tablecloth and we were all sitting around, the children, to have dinner. Father wasn't there because he came later, he always had his dinner by five o'clock, by himself. But we children, one o'clock was dinner with a white tablecloth. You see, the *yellow* tablecloth we used only for breakfast. Anyway, through the window we were always watching if a customer comes into the store. Always somebody came. My mother said, "You know children, the best thing is to eat all day. If we're going to eat all day, we're going to have customers all day." So we had every single day, I remember, always meat on the table, and soup. Always a nice dinner. And I'm not talking about Saturdays when there was no question about it, but every single day. It was a beautiful home, with everything on schedule. How many homes were there, you think, in small towns, where they had meat every day?

Every Thursday my mother and the maid started the baking. My father always sent from the mill to our house two big bags of flour, a hundred kilograms each, a man used to deliver it with a horse and wagon. Two big bags, I remember, were standing all the time in a little room we had, like a shed. You think you could just go out and buy ready-made everything you needed? Most things you had to bake yourself. Thursdays my mother would bake little matzos for the soup, cookies, bread and eggloaf — challa. Friday night everybody had to have challa to make a blessing, so you know how many challas she baked? And not only for us. Every Saturday the beggars came. We had Jewish beggars in the town who came every Saturday morning for a slice of challa. Usually people gave them just plain bread, but my grandparents owned the flour mill so at our place the beggars got slices of challa. A whole morning they were coming, the beggars. Some of them were very decent people, but poor.

And my mother had yet special extra people who got also a piece of cake or a few cookies. I remember Friday, before it started to get dark, my mother used to send me with food to a woman, her name was Rizele, an elderly widow, she had a retarded son. My mother helped her in other ways too. At home, with our big family, we hired a woman to come do a big washing three times a year. We didn't wash every day because the facilities weren't like you have here, you see. We had big wooden pots, three yards in diameter with wide bands of steel around them and the water wasn't dripping, they were made so good. Occasionally we would wash stockings or a little dress but big washings were sheets, pillowcases, white shirts — my brothers every single day put on a white shirt and with a hard collar — and there was lots of linen. My mother was nuts about linen, don't ask how much we had there. Lots. That hired woman came usually by four o'clock in the morning and we soaked all the white things: towels, tablecloths, shirts, sheets. She washed for three days and every night she went home not before ten. We had a special pressing machine, a hand one, not electric, that used to always crack the buttons of my brother's shirts and I remember for days I was sewing, this was my job. My mother was busy in the store and a household like ours, even with the maid, was a full-time job so she used to bring that woman, Rizele, with the retarded son, to help with the mending. Let's say a sheet got ruined, she put a patch, or some shirts needed seaming, you know, after a big wash like this she worked, imagine, three days to mend everything. So she always came with that son and when we had dinner, my mother always fed that boy too. He must have been in his early twenties, he couldn't even talk loud, wherever his mother went, he went, such a gentle boy, retarded but he didn't do anybody any harm, and maybe he wasn't retarded. They were killed later, Rizele and her son. Sure, the Germans took right away the retarded people, the poor. I remember one girl, she was a little crazy, they took her right away. They took away that man who was the water-carrier, he was also a little bit retarded. As soon as the Germans walked in, they took away these people and they vanished. Nobody knew where. Anyway, every Friday my mother gave me in a pot gefilte fish, soup, some chicken, and a whole challa, and she told me, "When you go into Rizele's house, you look around nobody should see you so she won't be ashamed that you bring her food." You know, she wasn't a beggar, she was just poor, she didn't have what to eat, with that son. I remember I went every Friday with food.

So can you imagine how many challas my mother had to bake? And they made butter cakes with cocoa inside, ah! It was delicious. And cookies, and strudels. On Thursday afternoon after dinner one o'clock, they started baking and didn't stop till Friday. So that's why I say we had a very nice home. Other people will tell you they didn't have what to eat, how they struggled, if they had once a week a piece of meat for the Sabbath, it was a good week.

But we had a good life. I'm telling you, all the children had a very good life. The only thing is that every day was similar to the other day.

I remember my brothers were always busy reading and learning. Just before the war Chamel started to learn French by himself. English he spoke already better than I do now. We had a relative in New York and two years before the war he came to visit his parents in Pinczow, so naturally he came to visit us. He heard Chamel speak English and he said, "If I wouldn't know that you are living here and you're born here, I would think you're an American."

My grandparents had a warehouse in Pinczow, bags of salt to sell wholesale, and Chamel was there the accountant, the bookkeeper. I don't think he earned some money for this. They bought him sometimes a gift or something. That was Europe, my dear. I think they made him a suit once. Never had anything from the grandparents, my mother's parents. They were very wealthy, but they never gave anything. My grandfather was the richest man in town. He also owned the local flour mill. But when he died, he didn't have a slice of bread. They didn't call their living-room a living-room, they called it a "salon." Beautiful. A special man came from Warsaw to make their floors. That was my mother's parents, and my father's parents lived in Lublin. My father was a very intelligent man, he was doing the book-keeping for Grandfather and he owned twenty percent of that flour mill, that's why he didn't work in our shoe store.

My brother Srulcie went upstairs every morning to work with the leather for shoes, for hours. He played the fiddle too. He wanted so much to play his fiddle and he never had the time but he practised anyway, for himself, whenever he had a second, a minute free. You know, he carried everything on his shoulders, that man, and he was so delicate, he had a heart of gold. He worked so hard upstairs like he would have a family at least of six children. He cared so much, with his whole soul. I remember he had always blisters on his fingers. He had to make sure that he cuts good the leather, the same thing like a butcher when he cuts meat, he has to be a good cutter to make money, and if you don't know how to cut meat, you lose money. You have to know your business. Srulcie was standing there days and nights in that room up there, at a cutting table, with a special knife for the hard leather to cut, and sometimes he would go to sleep three o'clock in the morning. Oh, he worked hard. And yet, any second he had to rest from work, he would grab the fiddle. He had a special tune, and you know how many times I wanted to remind myself that tune? I can't. One of these days it's going to come back to me. When he practised his fiddle and with his foot he was tapping, we heard everything downstairs because the ceiling was very thin. And this tune was so much ringing all the time in my ears, and I can't remind myself.

Then, at night, when he had a little bit of time, he was right away reading, he was such a reader. Both brothers. They never went to Polish public school because my parents were afraid if they're going to go there with the Gentiles, they would get spoiled or something. So they hired teachers to come give lessons to Chamel and Srulcie, I remember, for every subject came another professor.

I went to public school, mixed, Polish and non-Polish. It wasn't like a school here, it was just a little house with a few rooms and that's it. That was the whole school. What do you think, we had schools like you have it here? Are you kidding? I was thirteen when I finished but I was going already to another school, a really religious one, Beth Yaakov, learning Hebrew, Talmud, history, and only girls went there, no boys, but we had men teachers. I wanted to go farther in learning, but to go to college was out of the question because you had to go Saturdays and my parents were too religious. I cried, I wanted to go. No use. There was a college in Pinczow but only one Jew was going there, I remember, a boy, he was the only one, so people pointed their fingers because he's going on the Sabbath.

I don't know if the boys were better treated, all the children were treated equally, my parents loved each of us. Well, maybe in education, maybe they gave the men a better chance. They knew a girl is going to get married, and she doesn't need it. Maybe the boys were different treated, but it didn't feel like that, I felt my parents loved us all the same.

And I loved Israel. But at the beginning I wanted to get to know him, so I said we don't have to be serious, let's be friends, good friends. Why just right away say you're going to marry me? I knew that's so far, like from here to Hollywood. Let's be good friends first. But he was very jealous when I went to Lublin in the wintertime because he knew Leon was there, you know, and that I wanted to have a good time.

Israel always went back to Lodz, he only came for a couple months in the summertime and once in a blue moon for a week or so in the winter. It was very cold in Poland, and we were walking on the streets, I remember my eyes were frozen, it was so bitter cold. Well, we couldn't go to my house, my parents were there, so we used to go to the movie theatre, we were sitting there, we didn't look at a movie, we were just sitting somewhere to warm up. The man who owned that movie house, Kopcinski was his name, he knew already that we paid just to sit there, we didn't care about the movie, how many times can you see the same movie? Well, I supposed we smooched. But you could be sure we didn't smooch like they do here. Are you kidding? You had to be careful somebody shouldn't see. I remember that Kopcinski was always looking, he gave us such a smile, they're here again, they're paying for the ticket just to be somewhere. But I remember a movie, I saw it six times, it was out of this world. I think it's "The Good Earth," and Paul Muni played in it and I'll never forget, they built the first train, and what a joy it was when they saw the train going for the first time. It was a terrific movie.

But my parents made it so terrible for me for six years, that believe me, if we wouldn't have married later, I would have a nervous breakdown. They made it miserable for me. For no reason at all.

I always told them, "His family is even nicer than mine, what are you against?"

"Because he's an actor." They wanted only a rich man for me. I deserve a rich man.

I said, "Money is here today and tomorrow it could be somewhere else. I don't go for money!" They couldn't understand. I'm nuts, that's all. So I had a very tough time.

Every day, you know where I was writing letters to Israel? In the bathroom. And it was outside. There I was, sitting on that toilet, writing. I used to take perfume with me because I had to sit there and hour and a half and write the letters. I was reading there the letters from him and writing there the letters to him. So it wasn't a picnic, for six years. It was very hard. Every day he had a letter from me, and I had every day from him. You know how it goes with love letters. And I got the letters at the post office, what do you mean, a letter will come to the house?

"He's an actor."

"He isn't an actor. It's just a hobby."

No use.

I didn't find him interesting because I saw he was an actor. No, I always said to myself, if I'm going to get married, it has to be someone with character. It's something you're born with, that's what I thought, and I think so now too. Character, it's in you, you cannot teach somebody to be a person, if you aren't, it's too bad, that's the way you are. I saw Israel has got character, he's a *mensch*, human, and that's what I liked the most. And Leon, I saw he hasn't got, and I didn't make a mistake, he doesn't.

Well, I don't know what I was thinking that time of doing with my life, but that was the life. What did I want? I don't know, not exactly. You know what? In Europe, a nineteen-year-old girl is so naïve, at that time, so naïve, as much you think, it's not enough. Very naïve in Europe. I was thinking I'm probably going to be in the shoe business. But when I met Israel already, so I had plans. The plans were, if they will allow me to marry him, maybe I'll go to a big city. I always liked a big city. I wanted to go to Lodz, with Israel, but that was a dream.

⤳ ISRAEL ⤳

I haven't changed. Well, I don't believe in people any more, people are looking only for their own egoism, only for themselves, don't care for anybody, as long as they have what they want. After I went through so much, I saw that people are just a bunch of animals, don't care for each other nothing at all, just for the nearest people to them, and if they have to have it, they always say, "I want," and in the meantime they're hurting people, but saying "I want." Now I'm sure of it. Nearly everybody is like this. My character didn't change, my thought changed. I haven't changed. I just look skeptical on the whole world.

I can tell you with a Talmudic parable, to understand. A king once was running away from a revolution. He ran to a village to a farmer, a Jewish farmer.

"Listen, some revolutionaries are running after me and want to kill me because I am the king."

The farmer said, "What can I do?"

"Can you hide me?" asked the king.

The farmer said, "Yes, I can hide you."

It used to be in the olden times that instead of mattresses they had straw covered with a sheet. So the farmer said, "I can put you in under the straw and cover you with the sheet."

The king said, "That's all right."

And the farmer covered him.

It didn't take long, the revolutionaries came in. They had rifles with bayonets. They pushed the bayonets into the straw everywhere, to see if somebody's there. Nothing happened. And they went away.

The king was there a few days and the revolution was crushed. When he went out from that Jewish farmer's place, he said, "I will never forget you, what you did for me."

When the king became king and everything was normal, after half a year, the farmer reminded himself that the king promised to give him something for saving his life. The farmer went to the palace, they didn't let him in. But he had a piece of paper from the king, he showed the paper, they showed it to the king.

"Oh, yes! Let him in. That's my saviour."

The farmer came in, it was an elegant palace, and the king was sitting on his chair.

"Yes, my dear, what can I do for you?"

The farmer said, "Dear King, you told me that whatever I'll ask you will give me. It has been bothering me so long, I can't sleep. Just one single thing I want to know, for my philosophy: tell me how did you feel when the revolutionaries came in, and pushed their bayonets into the straw where you were hiding. How did you feel? That's what I want to know."

Naturally, the king got mad.

He said, "For embarrassing me, in the presence of so many people, about how I was hidden, I pronounce on you a sentence of death."

The farmer said, "Dear King," and he cried and started to beg.

But the king said, "Nothing will help because embarrassing the king in a public place is the worst crime. And not only that, I'll hang you myself."

The farmer cried, he begged, nothing helped. The king ordered to put up a scaffold with a rope. It took two days and they came to the king and said, "Your honour king, your gracious king, it's ready."

He said, "Yes? Take out that farmer."

They took the farmer, put him on the scaffold and the hangman put the rope on his neck, and the king said, "My privilege and pleasure will be I'll hang him myself."

They tied the knot on the farmer's neck, and the king went

out to the scaffold, took the farmer's face in his hands, and whispered in his ear, "Like this I felt."

The king took off the rope and he said, "My dear friend, how could I verbally give you to understand how it was when I was hiding and the bayonets were pushed in the straw? I could not. But now you know exactly how I felt."

I was born in 1920. My mother died when she was around twenty-two years old. I was nine months old. She went to do a good deed on a Friday night and took a little bit of soup, bread, and meat to give to a poor neighbour. It was in the wintertime and she wanted to give the food hot so she kept it under the coat. When she was walking, it was slippery and she fell backwards. Split her head.

I didn't have a stepmother yet, Father didn't remarry till a few years later, but I already had one brother, Chaim-David, three years older than me, and Father could not work and take care of us at the same time. So my brother and me left Father in Lodz and went to live with my father's parents in Pinczow.

I remember there I learned anti-Semitism when I was seven years old. I came to school the first time and after a few weeks the principal came into the class and the teacher wanted to show off so he asked me to write down how much is four times five, three times six, two times nine. I wrote it all down on the blackboard. The principal also asked me to write clearly my own name. I did it and the teacher was very proud of me. After school — there were two Jewish children and fifty non-Jewish — when we went out all the other children hit me because I was nearly the best in school, every question I answered, and the teacher showed off. They hit me and I came home bleeding.

We Jewish kids were smarter in school not because Jews are smarter but because we were already learning in the Jewish school, the yeshiva, philosophy, logic, and history from five years old, so what was it for us to know how to write your name or five times six? Nothing.

I remember once, I was eight years old, a bunch of us went swimming, had fun, and we forgot the time and missed school. We went running to the yeshiva and sat down in the classroom to learn. The teacher came in, he did not open his mouth, nothing. We got worried. Then, quietly, he just went to the corner, took out a fiddle, and started to play and to sing. And even though that could only happen once in a thousand yeshivas, it was such a beautiful incident, it stays with me in memory and reminds me how opposite I felt in the Polish public school. For example, I was also a good soccer player. When I was in third grade, the seventh grade asked me to come to play with them. They didn't ask me, they called me, "Hey, you, dirty Jew, come, you're going to play with us. We need you." And if I would say no, they would hit me. That was my lessons.

My father remarried, to a cousin. My grandparents loved us so much they didn't want to give me and my older brother back to my father, but we went. Me and my brother were already ten and thirteen years old, it's a lot of years, so when we came to Father's house in Lodz, we were strange, we were sitting in the corner. I cried all the time, "I want to go back home." Till the last day till the war I never said Lodz is my home. When I said, "I'm going home," home was Pinczow. I was very attached to my grandfather and grandmother. I loved them dearly.

My grandfather was a tall man with a very small beard, like a goat. So much joy I remember, so many jokes. I have to tell you an incident that happened when I was a boy in Pinczow. Before the war, the stores had to be closed at seven o'clock and if a policeman caught you five minutes past seven he gave you a fine. Once my grandfather forgot the time exactly, the customer was still there and till my grandfather gave him change and went out to close the store, it was five minutes past seven. The police was right there and gave him a fine for more than he made in the whole day. My grandfather says he's going to go to court for it, he's not going to pay. He was a very smart man, shrewd like a lawyer.

When he came back from court, he sat down and said, "Children, it is to laugh how many hours it took to show them how stupid they are."

The judge called him up: "Mr Rubinek, why did you not close the store at seven o'clock?"

And he said, "Your Honour, I did close exact at seven o'clock."

"But the policeman has written down it was five minutes past seven," the judge said.

"Your Honour, may I prove it?"

"If you can," says the judge. "I don't know how."

"Your Honour," my grandfather said, "here in this court is probably forty, fifty people. I would ask you, your Honour, and everybody to take out their watches to see if all of them are the same time."

Naturally, most were not: five minutes here, ten minutes there.

And my grandfather said, "As you see, your Honour, on my watch was seven o'clock, on the policeman's watch was five minutes past seven, and on your watch, your Honour, it would be five minutes before seven. So…"

The judge stood up, "Mr Rubinek, case dismissed."

Such a man was my grandfather. He died in 1935.

We have a distinguished family. My middle name, Zishe, is from my great-great-great-great-grandfather who was one of the greatest rabbis in Poland. They called him Rebbe Rab Zishe. If you say to any Chassidic Jew, "Rebbe Rab Zishe," he knows who it is. To give you an example, I have a friend whose son is very religious and buys all those books about the rabbis, and when I said that I am tracing my name back to Rebbe Rab Zishe, he opened his mouth and he sat down and he couldn't move.

I'll tell you my thoughts. It's very important for me, my background, as a human being, where and who I come from. When I'm sitting by myself, I want to understand what is going on around me, how people live, cheat, only for their own "I," for their own welfare, and don't care who you are and who they themselves are, and I'm closing my eyes and I start to think from where I come, who I am, to help me live and be a better human man. If I would tell you that your father was a dealer in white slaves, and your grandfather was a murderer, and your great-grandfather was a leader of the Mafia — a nice heritage — would you care who they were? I mean to say, if that was my family, I would hide my heritage, and maybe I would even convert, to forget all my past. But I have no reason for it. All my family, on both sides, was always the highest notch. I'm not talking richness. Intelligent, always did good for other people. Learned. Decent. Nice. People looked up to them. I have an obligation to them. And I have an obligation to those people that went to death for no reason at all, only because they were born Jewish.

In a way, I'm bitter. But I wouldn't take advantage of anybody. Or revenge.

For Frania, it's a story. And for me, it's living over. That's the difference. She tells you a story how it happened, but I live it over, again and again. I feel I'm there. For me, if I'm telling you what happened, I live with my body, with my thought, over, over again. I could yell now, I could. I saw with my own eyes how the Poles were so enjoying their life when the Germans killed the Jews, they were just joyful, for no reason at all. I have a conception that, if not for the Christian world, there would not be a single Jew on earth today. Maybe there would be just somebody, a few fanatics who would stay and hold on to it. The Christian world pushed you away, pushed you into the corner, put you in ghettos, and that made me a stronger Jew. I would not convert. I would maybe if I lived with the Poles like brothers and sisters, just that my religion is different from them and that's all, maybe I would feel no difference. But there never was one single hundred years without killing, I could show you black and white.

I'll tell you, when I came to this country, to Canada, I under-

stood why there's so many mixed marriages. Because the truth
is, here the people are living more together with the Jews, with
more friendship than in Europe. There's more Christian con-
verts to Judaism than Jews to Christianity. And because they
live together as neighbours in good harmony, it's not a big thing
to get married to the neighbour's daughter. And if the trend
wouldn't be cut off, if the hate will be cut off, or if Pope John
XXIII would be alive and would make a big revolution in the
dogma of the Christian world, it could be that the Jews would
assimilate more. But it happens that we always were pushed
away, by the best ones even. That's why in Europe the belief of
Jewishness was stronger and stronger. You take me, I am not a
religious man, I'm not an atheist, but if you will come to me
right now with a gun and tell me that I should convert, if not
you'll kill me, with the greatest happiness I would give my life.
I have nothing against me to deny myself. I have nothing against
my Jewishness. I know we didn't do anything wrong. And I
would never be a traitor to my nation, because I have a responsibility to my nation, because their blood is my blood, blood
that's now in the earth, and I have a responsibility not to run
away from them, because they were killed for no reason at all.

My father used to say, "If you deny something, be sure you
know what it is you're denying." He used to say, "Know — and
deny. But don't deny when you don't know."

My father was a very highly scholared, a very highly learned,
a philosophical man. He was also an arbitrator between people
who had quarrels in business or family. Between Jewish people,
if there was a quarrel, it was never decent to go to an official
Gentile court, they always went to a respectable, understanding
man, to straighten them out. So they came to my father. When I
came back to live with him after my grandparents, it just made
me proud to see how people used to come to him with so much
respect and stood with open mouths to hear what he would say.
He had a sharp mind, capable of anything. He was educated in
Yiddish and in Hebrew, and he used to sit till two, three o'clock

in the morning studying Jewish mysticism, numerology — cabal-ism. He had a corner in the house with his books, and when he sat down, nothing else in the world could interest him because he was so deep in mysticism. There were only a few people he could talk to. The truth is, he looked down on a lot of people because he considered that they didn't know what they were talking about. And when he talked in his cabalistic, philosoph-ical way, it was only with his friends. His children, he thought, were too young to understand him.

The oldest son was Chaim-David who used to write poetry. Once when he was a small boy he copied down all the songs of *King Solomon* on a postcard. It was just beautiful and readable. He was learned, handsome, good-natured, and we got along very well.

The next oldest was me. Then from my stepmother, my half-brothers and sisters: Yitzchak, born 1925, if he were alive he would be sixty-three years old now. Later was Sarah, nine years old when the war broke out. Then was Chiel, two years younger, and Reuven, Chayaleh, and the twins Rachmiel and Toba. It was a lovely family, six boys and three girls. You never saw in your life such beautiful children.

When I was small somebody took me once to see theatre and I didn't understand what I saw but it stayed with me. When I got older, I put my sidecurls under my hat and I went by myself to see a movie for the first time. Al Jolson in *The Jazz Singer*. I was sitting and crying, it really made on me an impression. Then I went to see *Mata Hari* with Greta Garbo and Ramon Novarro.

The thing is, we were living just two houses away from one of the biggest movie theatres in Lodz. In 1936, a cowboy from Hollywood came to Poland. Tom Mix. Probably half the city was running to see him. Mostly we saw in Poland cowboy pictures. Believe it or not. I remember Fred Thomson, Tom Mix, Ken Maynard, Buck Jones. So Tom Mix came to Lodz in person in a cowboy uniform, with the pants, with the big hat, and half a city came running to the Corso Theatre on Zielona Street number six. So Tom Mix stood and talked in English and nobody understood him.

I was going to yeshiva in that time and we were learning about Joseph in Egypt. Came to my mind how beautiful it would be to put that story on the stage. I came home and wrote down a script and I directed and produced *The Sale of Joseph in Egypt*. Also I played Joseph.

When I was fifteen, I finished yeshiva and without telling my father I went to a Jewish drama school. A lot of my friends were composers, musicians, actors, singers, writers, all creative people. None of us were professionals. Somebody told us about an organization that had an amateur theatre group so we paid a few zlotys and became members. It turned out to be a Jewish socialist group that called themselves the "Bundt" but they were not Zionists and also not Communists. Their dogma was to fight for socialism in the country of their birth. I saw, a lot of us saw, that the anti-Semitism is so great that it would be just impossible to work with the Poles together and I never really belonged to the Bundtist party. I wanted just to play theatre, not to talk politics.

At the drama school they didn't let you play right away anyway. First of all the director gave lectures on how to talk clearly. In the Yiddish language, Lithuanians spoke different from Ukrainians and in Poland there were many strange dialects so we were taught to talk uniformly: one type of Yiddish. They taught you how to speak a monologue, to be able to project to the last row in the theatre, not to eat your words, how to turn, how to walk on the stage, not to talk with your back to the audience — I remember that was absolute. You could talk with your back only rarely, because it was disrespectful to the audience. We did a lot of Yiddish plays by Peretz, Sholom Aleichem — I played once *Tevye the Dairyman* — Hirschbein, Leivick, some Russian plays in Yiddish and sometimes we wrote ourselves one-acts. I did very well and I became later a director too.

In 1938, Paul Wagner, the great German actor, came to Lodz

and he gave a concert about how hands talk. I was amazed to see, to hear him. He said, "An actor is an artist and a true artist has to be sensitive to everything around him. If he is not sensitive, with good intentions, understanding the most he can of everybody, then he is no artist. When an actor plays he is not himself alone, he was to feel and think like someone else so he is forced to understand other people and be compassionate to the world around him." Till now his words stay with me.

A lot of people were jealous of me and my friends because we always went to theatre together, parties, night-clubs, everywhere together and we had a decent, nice life, nice youth. I cut off my sidecurls when I was fifteen years old. The climate of the time for us was to break away, not from tradition, but from the religious point of view. We didn't want to be fanatical like our parents so we started to understand another life, cut off the sidecurls, shave, learn how to dance, how to enjoy life a little bit.

My friend Henek Krowitski had a brother who came from France who knew how to dance "salon" dances. He taught his brother and his brother taught us. We rented a room for ourselves, everybody put in money, not to bother the parents. Once we were singing and playing there and it was so nice that half the street was listening to us. We used to spend all our free times in that room. When I was sixteen, when we went dancing in a club, I was already one of the best dancers. We had mandolins and we used to practise at home with girls, privately. I had my mandolin till the last minute. I think that in the ghetto later my father sold the mandolin for bread.

But we kids didn't break away in a big way. Traditionally, we prayed every day and kept the Sabbath at home. We weren't beatniks. First of all, we were all dressed elegant, to the last money. That was the trend. We used to discuss Dostoevsky, Tolstoy, Chekhov, politics, anti-Semitism, who was right, who was not right about psychology, about the philosophy of life, of religion. The general consensus was that religion, like the Fascist countries, had too much power. And the most talk was of art, not to be satisfied just with working but to be a creator.

I did not want my father to know I am playing theatre, it would have hurt him very much. When he saw I cut off my sidecurls he didn't like it a bit. No big discussion, he just said, "I don't like it, what's going to become of you?"

The truth is, he was scared I will become a Communist and Communism is anti-religious. He didn't trust me. And he was scared I would influence his other kids.

Once I had a performance to make at eight o'clock. I was at home at a traditional Friday-night dinner and it was not conceivable to leave everybody in the middle of the meal and go away. But I had no choice, I had to be at the performance and I could not tell that I'm playing theatre. So I had to just break away in the middle of singing, I got up and went out. I came home probably two o'clock in the morning, my father stopped talking to me for quite a few weeks — the worst thing he could do to me because I respected him very much. Playing theatre was to him the lowest thing. Why? He was thinking in theatre there is more freedom to go away altogether from decency.

One time I was very proud of him. He finally found out about me when a friend of his came and told him I was an actor and that he himself had seen me in the theatre. When I came home from playing, my father stood up and faced me with the facts.

He said, "But if he was really a friend, he wouldn't tell me. That means that he told me to hurt me so I didn't give him the satisfaction, I just asked him if you spoiled anything or did you play good."

Then I got even more respect for my father when he asked me quietly to explain what I was doing.

"Father," I said, "every human being is for himself and thinks that anything wrong or good only happens to him, to nobody else. If husband and wife are fighting quietly at home, they think that nobody has those troubles, only them. Theatre creates those situations and shows the people that nobody's alone, everybody can have the same troubles but everybody solves those problems by himself." That was an occasion.

When I was sixteen years old, I had to learn a trade. My father sold hardware wholesale and in one night he was robbed of everything. He came in the morning to the store, there was nothing left. He wasn't insured so that day we became poor. He opened another hardware store, a small one, it didn't go good, so he started to sell coal by the pound. And I had to learn a trade to help out and whatever I made I brought back because there were quite a few kids at home.

In an intelligent home it was never conceived that a boy or girl should go be a tailor or a shoemaker. It was always nicer to have a trade that has to do with thinking because in Poland, mostly ignoramuses who didn't know how to read or write became bakers, shoemakers. A little bit higher was a tailor. But in an intelligent home, it was considered philosophically that a tailor is a servant, he has to pat you, go around you and take your measure and it was not considered smart to be somebody's serviceman.

My stepmother's parents had a factory where they used to make socks and when we got robbed my stepmother bought a machine to make socks in the house. I looked how she was working, I understood the principles of knitting and I went into a factory to learn the knitting trade. At least that had to do with thinking, with doing designs. Always you had to create.

After they robbed us, we couldn't afford where we lived so we moved to just one big room and a kitchen, that's all. Very poor. Two brothers to a bed.

I bought an old knitting machine for fifty zlotys, that means for five dollars, brought it home, worked at it, put it together and made that machine go. I could have sold it for five hundred dollars. I taught my older brother Chaim-David and my younger brother Yitzchak to work at home on that machine. My older brother was so delicate that if he would have gone out to work at a job and somebody would yell at him, he would faint. A whole day long he was in books, and writing. He could have been a very big poet. My younger brother Yitzchak was so handsome, so good, he went to yeshiva and he came home to work all night on the machine. My mother was at home with the children and she worked in the store also. Besides a knitter, I was a mechanic. I used to go like a doctor to fix machines all over, even when I was young, and there was no schooling for that, you had to learn by yourself.

Once a man came to me and asked if I would be able to work, he has only two machines, he can't pay much. A Jewish man, he was a bit deaf but very nice. I said why not. Work was slack then so I went to work for him, made sweaters and he used to go out and sell them, not much, but just enough to make a living. To make a living, that's a difficult thing to say. He had bread, butter, and three days in the week meat. That's all he had. I made fifty zlotys a week and for that could live a family of three. Not live — eat. Later on he took another man in, also a Jewish man but he was older than me. He was showing off that he was a socialist, that he believed in the Communists, that he liked the Russian regime.

After a few weeks working he said, "I'm going to ask for a raise."

I looked at him like crazy. "Why a raise? You see the owner is not making enough money even as it is."

He said, "Are you keeping with the bourgeoisie?"

I said, "No, but it has to be with logic. I know how much it costs him and he hasn't even sold all his merchandise. How could you ask for a raise? He's a poor man, not a big manufacturer, just a small man."

So he started to yell, plain yell at me. "I'm going to sue him for not paying overtime!"

We were working from eight o'clock to eight o'clock, that was a normal day's work. Sometimes till ten but we could go away whenever, the owner never demanded overtime. Anyway he sued him for not paying overtime and I was so outraged and so mad that I went as a witness against my co-worker. And he lost.

That gave me a lesson not to belong to any party. We thought about the Communists like this: they would like to share, that means the taking, not the giving. They liked to share what somebody else has. The party told the member that when socialism comes, he would share in all the richness. That they liked. That means they didn't like to work to have but to have what somebody else has. Any party member never thought for himself, somebody else was thinking for him.

I had a friend who came from an intelligent home but not religious. He didn't have a father, just sisters and a mother. His name was Shmulek Berek. Like me, he was also a knitter. He was not specially artistic and in our circle he was more a bystander. I remember once I was working in a factory and my friend Shmulek came to me and said, "My sisters have jobs but they're not making enough. I am not working and I just don't feel good coming home to eat when I have nothing to contribute." In that time I was working from six in the morning till ten at night, it was peak season. I told him I'll work from six till two and give him the work from two till ten. I needed the money too but I didn't tell Father and that whole season I gave him half my work. We were to each other like brothers.

A peculiar thing happened, life is a puzzle for everybody. I met Shmulek in refugee camp after the war and I just couldn't move when I saw him alive. I fell on him, kissed him and I couldn't talk because I'm very sensitive, I had to cry. I'll never forget as long as I live, he stood like a mummy, didn't cry, just looked at me. I asked him to come into the house, he didn't want to. He didn't ask me what I'm doing, nothing, he talked for a little while, I asked him where he's going, he said he had a sister in Australia. And he went away and I never heard of him again. It bothers me till now. After so many years together, suddenly to become so cold, I'll never understand this. The surprise was for me how people change. I consider myself a thinking man and I don't think I changed. Mostly people don't know what they are. I know who I am. I was always naïve. When I gave Shmulek my work I didn't do it to get something out of it. I was pitying him because he hasn't got a father. And he said so humanly, "I don't think I should share food when I have nothing to contribute." So I helped him. And when we met after such a holocaust — he didn't have family left, nobody — when I met him, he was so cool, like a fish. As long as I'm going to live, he's going to stay in my eyes.

Summer was slack season for knitting so I went every summer to Pinczow to be with my grandparents and my two aunts. Pinczow is more than six hundred years old and it used to be one of the most important cities in the whole of Poland. The kings were there and in that city was the centre of the fighting between Protestants and Catholics. Eventually it became highly Catholic. But it went down and down in prestige till in the thirties it was a small town of not more than four thousand families. For me, to be in Pinczow in the summertime was like a vacation. One summer I fell in love with Frania. She always says she saw me first but I saw her before. Whenever I came, I saw her and I never had the guts to go talk to her. I wanted a date but I was always thinking maybe she will say no. In Lodz I didn't go out with anybody, I didn't have a special girl, I was not experienced. But in Pinczow, when her brother wanted me to teach dancing. I arranged he should bring his sister and the truth is, Frania was dancing the best. I danced with her to show how it should be done and we fell in love.

After that we made dates. Hidden and secret. I didn't know about her parents but I had my problems too. My grandfather died the year before so I had to answer to my grandmother and my two aunts. But when they found out I was dating a girl from a nice family they weren't too grouchy about it. We dated in the summer, then I had to go back to Lodz and I was lonesome, I wrote letters, as many as I could. It was a big love. She couldn't write to my address and I couldn't write to hers so she used to write me care of a friend of mine and I wrote letters "Poste Restante," which means they kept the letters at the post office till she came to ask for them.

I couldn't tell my father about it. Everything was supposed to be by matchmakers. One time a manufacturer came to my father's house, showed me a piece of a sweater and asked if I can make that design. His eyes popped out when I said yes. He said, "Okay, I'll leave you the sweater. Make a sample." When he came back and saw I made it, he was so glad, he asked me how much I would want per sweater. In that time a quarter of a zloty was a lot but when I saw he was so impressed, I said, "One zloty." And I could make in that time twenty-five sweaters a day. That means just a dream — twenty-five zlotys a day. He said no but he will make me the manager and the headmaster of his factory for a hundred zlotys a month. Beside that he will pay me whatever I make by piecework. And he will keep me all year round, including slack season. The point was, he had a daughter. He was Jewish. He told my father he would like to have me for a son-in-law for his only daughter. She was a blonde. She was the book-keeper there in the factory but I never really noticed her because I was already in love with Frania.

My father came to me and he went around the bush talking all kinds of things till finally he said, "I have a match for you."

I said, "I have to tell you the truth, it's too late. I have already."

He was speechless. He had sharp eyes, he didn't say a word, just looked. That made me feel bad when he just looked straight in my eyes.

After a few minutes he said, "May I know at least who it is?" I got red and told him. He said, "Without parents' consent? Not asking me? Not asking her father?"

I said, "I met her, talked to her and we gave each other our word." And a word is for me like a signature.

He said, "Nothing can help?"

I answered, "Nothing in the world."

Later on he was invited to a wedding in Pinczow. It happened

Frania was there and my aunt told him who was who. So he looked at her. Nobody could stand his hard eyes. He had two black beautiful eyes. Sharp like an eagle. Kind but sharp. He said to my aunt, "It's a beautiful girl," but to me he never said a word. Nothing.

Israel
I wanted only Frania and I was jealous of everybody. I didn't know Leon was after her. That she told me later. I was jealous of something else altogether. Why she lets them matchmake her with somebody from the town Wislica.

Frania
Now what is he talking? But I never went. I never said a word. I never even went to see him.

Israel
She told me, verbally, that they were matchmaking her with a rich guy and he wanted to give — right? — ten thousand zlotys to her parents.

Frania
Yes.

Israel
And he came to the store to see her.

Frania
I'm sorry. Not "he came." What's the matter with you? I never saw him in my life.

Israel
You told me he was fat.

Frania
No, no … Israel you're mixing up. A man came from Kato-wice in that time.

Israel
You didn't tell me from Wislica? The fat one?

Frania
No, I never saw him in my life.

Israel
That's what she told me.

Frania
I'm sorry.

Israel
Those things I remember better.

Frania
No.

Israel
But okay, let be like you say, you never met him.

Frania
I never met him in my life. Are you kidding?

Israel
His father came to look at her and he liked her right away.
And he wanted to give ten thousand zlotys.

Frania
His *father* came, yes, I didn't even know it's his father, but
I never saw *him*.

Israel
Then how do I know he was fat?

Frania
Because he is alive. Maybe after the war, somebody told
me, or told you that he's fat. I never saw him in my life.

Israel
How do you know he is alive?

Frania
Someone told me. Such a long time ago I don't remember.

Israel

She told me that he was fat, with a round face, a red round face, that's what she told me.

Frania

No, that was the man from Katowice. The one that wrote the letter, what's the matter with you? I could see him right now, this man.

Israel

In that man I wasn't jealous. I was jealous on the other thing, why she let herself be talked in — I didn't let myself talk to nobody. She told me that he came in and they were talking about it. I don't know what she said there. She told *me* she said "no," but what she said at *home* she didn't tell me. She told me also about a salesman that wanted her.

Frania

Oh, the salesman.

Israel

I was jealous of everybody. Her uncle Meyer wanted her. Her uncle Leon wanted her. She knew another man in Lublin, he wanted her — right?

Frania

So?

Israel

The main thing I was the lucky guy. And the main thing, my wife, if we're gonna live another fifty years, she still will be sorry. I am not sorry. So. What can I tell you? I'm still in love with my wife, after forty years. Every day is for me like yesterday I got married.

Frania

Oh my God!

Israel

And it's true, absolutely true. But I can't go around and yell all day long: I love you! I love you! It's going to be, like too weak. Soft. Has no sense to it.

Frania

I'm going to sing you that little song, "Twenty-five years I baked for you, if this is not love, then what is it?"

Israel

I cannot go around like other people and say: "sweetheart," and "honey." Everybody that came into our house in Montreal, and here in Ottawa, whoever in front of a few people calls his wife "Honey" — is something wrong at home. All right, it's not necessarily true, but how many couples when they're sitting at the table with other people — I showed it to my dear wife, and let her say if it's not true — they're calling: "Honey, sweetheart," and at home they are fighting like cat and mouse. I don't do it. I am enough emotional.

Frania

That's for sure.

Israel

I am not doing anything wrong, and if I do something wrong is without my knowledge. You have the best mother in the world, and I have the best wife in the world. And I am sure, Saul, after my death you will find out what kind of parents you had. But I wouldn't be able to enjoy it. The same thing as I am sorry now that I didn't give my father more pleasure. And that's what will happen.

꼭꼭 *FRANIA* ꘏꘏

I'll tell you what happened to me. My brothers had a friend, Shloime Zielony, a very intelligent boy, his father was a teacher.

So this Shloime, a handsome boy, used to drop by our house all the time. If you knew somebody very well in Pinczow, you came by any time of the day, without invitation. I hear in Israel it's the same style. He came over all the time, he liked me very much. One day my parents told me that Shloime Zielony knows in Wislica, a small town near us, a lovely family, they own a clothing store, they have a son, an only child, who is in the business too and this would be a terrific match for me. Shloime knew that we weren't rich and he said that these people would even pay my parents money to have me for a daughter-in-law. But I was going with Israel and I didn't want to even hear about it. They wanted me at least to go and see him, Shloime Zielony would arrange it. He would write a letter that the boy should come to my house or I should go to their house, the parents would go out of the room and leave us to talk. This was already modern. Otherwise they make the match and the kids don't know a thing. My parents thought maybe if I see this boy in Wislica with the good clothing business I'll get cold feet and leave Israel stand. So I said no, I'm not interested. Why should I turn somebody else's head in circles when I know I'm already in love?

Once came into the store a man and asked for a pair of shoes. It just happened Shaindele was serving him, not me. But I was so used to the shoe business I could tell the customer's size right away just by looking so I said, "Give him an eight and a half." In the meantime he started to talk to Shaindele, he said he's just passing through Pinczow, he's from Katowice, small talk. She gave him a pair of eight and a half, it fit perfect and he bought not one but three pairs of shoes. That was a big sale in that time, you didn't sell every day so many shoes. So I wrapped them and he paid and left. After a few days comes a letter to my parents from this man that he was in the store, he comes from Katowice, he gives his family name and who he is, from what parents he comes and everything plus he's proposing that he wants one of the daughters to marry, he likes her very much. But he wants not the daughter that served him but the one that wrapped the parcel. I'm telling you, we laughed. In a way, I felt a little bad but I turned it around and said to Shaindele, "See, he was right away smart to notice I'm older than you." But she wasn't that stupid. Anyway we laughed so hard and I don't even remember to this day if we answered the letter. Look, first of all, my parents weren't interested themselves in a man who just walks in from the blue. Secondly, they knew that if I refused that boy from Wislica where they wanted to pay ten thousand zlotys to have me for a daughter-in-law, why would I suddenly want this man from Katowice who bought three pairs of shoes?

I saw Israel's father and he saw me, only once, just a year before the war. My girlfriend got married and Israel's father came to Pinczow for the wedding because he happened to be a very good friend of my girlfriend's father. The wedding was in the house, they were serving a big dinner and there were long tables. So Israel's father was sitting there, he had a pair of eyes, when he looked at you, you got frightened. The eyes were just like pins and you felt the pins going right through you, such black burning eyes did he have. Smart eyes, he was some man, his father. I just felt, wherever I went, I had those two eyes on me because he knew that Israel has a girl in Pinczow. I suppose he asked somebody and he knew it's me. Whenever I looked, there were those two eyes. That was the first time we saw each other and it turned out to be the last time too.

I had such respect for my parents, especially Father, he was such a good man. My mother was a hard person a little bit. She was a little tough character, she could tell you something to really hurt your feelings. Not Father. She was strict but Father was the gentlest man. You know what? Israel is just like Father. He wouldn't hurt anybody's feelings, never. Listen, you live with a man so many years, it's not a day. So he's stubborn but everybody has something, you, me, who's perfect? And if he wasn't stubborn, would we be alive today? But the main thing is that he's good, he's got a heart of gold. To do a favour, he's not going to walk but he's going to run. I knew I'm hurting my parents by going out with Israel whenever he came, because it was not a decent thing to go out with a boy but I couldn't help it. The right thing to do was to break up and not go out with a boy at all.

When Israel came in the summertime, every night after the store was closed, we used to make a rendezvous and my mother got so red on her chest, like fire, it was burning inside. But what could she tell me? I had to go. What were we doing? We were necking. But not what the girls do nowadays, you could be sure. Before if a girl wasn't a virgin, she could never marry. It's funny that in this world we're living now, if a girl's a virgin, they say oh, something wrong with her, nobody wants her.

My father used to tell us the story of the matchmaking between him and my mother. My mother's family lived in Pinczow and his family lived in Juzefow, another small village. So her side wanted to test the groom to see if he can learn the Talmud, if he knows something or if he's a nothing, and they arrived in his village in big style in a coach with horses. They were quite well-off, you see, compared to his family. But when they tested him about the Talmud, he was so smart he impressed the hell out of them and they said well, the bride and groom should meet somewhere to see if they like each other. They met in a hotel, in Warsaw. So my mother's mother must have been very sneaky, because she saw him carrying a little valise and she wanted to see what he has in there. So she sneaked in and what do you think she found in that valise? A little pocket-mirror. And you know what? It was almost the end of the match. A religious boy has a little mirror in his valise to look at himself? Let me tell you, that means old-fashioned. But the matchmaker came and said it's not a crime, so what if he wants to look at himself in a mirror, over this should end a match? And I suppose he started to talk a good talk and there was a match. But it almost was nothing because of that stupid mirror my grandmother found in the valise. A funny thing is that once she told me, "You know, with your grandfather I've been so long and everything but it was never a match."

❦ ISRAEL ❦

Matchmaking was a way of life. Even in my group of friends, though we were, let's say, a little more sophisticated, even so, the parents used to arrange marriages. But when a girl of our circle had to meet a boy, the rest of us went to look if it's good for her. When we said okay, it was a match. When we said we don't like him, she didn't like him either. The parents were supposed to know what's best for the children and the children were supposed to have the greatest respect for the parents. Naturally, the world doesn't always work that way.

We had a cousin in Pinczow, an intelligent man, but the family, whatever they made they spent. He had a son the whole area used to talk about. Intelligent, handsome, elegantly dressed, learned in Polish, in Yiddish, in everything. Since the family didn't have much money they were matchmaking that boy to the daughter of a man who owned a tavern. That man had to deal all day long with drunkards and his daughter was also staying there talking dirty with the customers and sometimes we heard she could even take a drunk by the neck and throw him out if he didn't pay. So the whole town was saying unbelievable, unbelievable, how can that be a match? He is so delicate, he couldn't even talk loud. And she is a mouthpiece. But nobody can tell nobody what to do. What happened is they got married and he had hell. She made him sit when she wanted him to sit and to be quiet when she wanted to talk. He never saw that in his life, his mother had so much respect for his father, so he got scared to go home to tell because he didn't want to embarrass his parents and divorce would be a scandal. Later on, during the war, he was separated finally from his wife by force when the Germans started deporting Jews to the camps. It was a terrible thing but we used to joke that he was the happiest guy probably to go with the deportation.

One friend, Zulkowski, from a very Chassidic family, fell in love with a girl, he didn't know she was not Jewish. She talked Yiddish but with a German accent. He took her into our circle and we liked her very much. Later on she told him she was not Jewish but German. He was shocked but still he was in love, I think. She promised him she would convert. So his parents accepted it even though they were very Chassidic people. Judaism doesn't have missionaries but if somebody wants wholeheartedly to convert, the Jewish law says they should be received with open arms. It very seldom happened but if it was a case like this, the convert was always more Jewish than a real Jew. A few weeks before the war, Zulkowski's girlfriend told him she knows what's going to happen to the Jews. As she is from German descent, she will take him and hide him. That was all right but he was asking also to hide his parents. She told him, "I don't care for them a bit, I care for you." It is a peculiar thing, here in America, the minute the children get older or married, a small wall comes between them and the parents — that is yours and this is mine. In Poland, with us, to the last day of life, the children, married or not, always for the parents had the greatest respect. I never sat on that chair where my father used to sit, not because he told me but the respect was so great, I wouldn't do it. So Zulkowski, even though he loved that girl so much, when he heard she wants to save just him, the connection between parents and children was so strong, he cut her off right away, he let her go and never saw her again. And it happened that he was killed by the Germans in the war.

ᴄᴛᴛ *FRANIA* ᴛᴛᴛ

Before the war, when it was Passover in our town, no Jewish soul you saw on the streets. It was Eastertime for the Gentiles and they go to church, I think for mass. They are reminded the Jews killed Jesus and a Jew knew that if he's going to be on the street, he's going to be beaten up, or he's not going to be alive any more. So we knew that before Passover was Easter and we don't go out.

Just before the war, maybe a year, the anti-Semites rented boys to picket outside Jewish stores not to let customers go in. I remember there was one boy, he was a dog-catcher, a nothing, a bum, and they paid him to stand at our store when it was a market day, on Tuesday and Friday. So when the farmers came, they were just very ordinary people, they wanted to come into the store, and that boy yelled, "What kind of a Catholic are you? Your money that you're sweating for, you're giving to the Jews?" So naturally, the farmer was shy, he walked away, and we saw we're going to lose all the business.

My brother Srulcie called the boy over: "How much did they pay you? Did they give you five zlotys? I'll give you ten. Stand there but don't talk. Stand, like a dummy." So he gave him money and he stood there but he didn't say anything. You know who that boy was? His father and mother were janitors at my grandparents' home.

There was always hate between the Jews and Poles, I cannot pin-point exactly why. There was such a big distance between us, they had big eyes, because the majority of stores were Jewish. So I suppose jealousy made the hate and I guess jealousy is a natural thing. The majority in Pinczow was Gentiles but they didn't have stores, they all worked in the government, for the city hall, or they were farmers. And the Jews, where are they going to work? They didn't let us work in government, they didn't let us own land, so we had stores. I'll tell you, my dear, life was no dream for a young girl in Pinczow.

⌒ *ISRAEL* ⌒

The Poles taught me how to hate them. We had to hide during Easter, we couldn't go out at night when they went to pray in church, specially in Pinczow. In small towns it was much more dangerous than big cities. My grandfather's house in Pinczow was connected one wall with the church and we closed ourselves very tightly, if not, whoever went out, if he didn't get killed, he came home with blood, because they were hitting and yelling, "Christ killer, Christ killer, Christ killer!" And the best Pole, the best of them, if he was a friend it was only because he could get something out of the Jew. And especially the government was anti-Semitic. You didn't pay taxes according to what you sold. For the Jews, they just made an estimate you should pay so much and it sometimes came out you didn't make all year what they asked you to pay. And you *had* to pay, if not they came in, threw out the bed with the chair with the table and sold it for you, for the tax.

The Polish farmers, the peasants, were anti-Semitic from the church. They were just plain religious people and couldn't stand that the Jews killed Lord Jesus Christ. Every single Sunday they were reminded about it. I have no good memories. None whatsoever.

I never hated anyone like I hated the Poles. I hate saying that, I know how it sounds, but I felt that way — I was forced. And today I have Polish people that I love. May I explain myself? Maybe, maybe there were some Poles who saved Jews in the war just for the sake of saving them but still they got a lot of money out of it, I'm sure. It was such a thing too that they saved some Jews for friendship. I never heard about it but I can't deny it, it must have happened. But I have an example for that. The Jewish law says that if you open an egg and it has in it a drop of blood, you cannot eat it. But the fact is, if I open sixty eggs, mix them, and two happen to have a drop of blood, you may eat them because those two eggs are vanishing between the sixty, so it comes out to nothing. The same thing, if in Poland was a few Poles who saved a few Jews, that's miraculous for the ones who lived but twenty-five to thirty percent more Jews could have been saved for sure if the Poles didn't go out and squeal on us. The Germans did not know who is a Jew and who not. The Poles recognized us. They were walking specially on streets looking people in the eyes and bringing them to the Germans, "This is a Jew."

Once during the war I asked a German, a plain soldier, why does he hate us so much? He said, "We hate you from the law, but the Poles hate you from their hearts." To tell the truth, I believed him. First of all, it was still in the Polish mind that the Jews are slaughtering a Christian child to make Passover matzos. I accuse the Catholic church. According to them, we are cursed for all time because we killed Jesus Christ and we don't want to recognize him as a God. That's the dogma.

Also, the jealousy. Seventy percent Poles were ignoramuses, I mean, did not finish any schooling, were farmers. The Jewish people were always able to write and read and the parents, even if they didn't have what to eat, did everything possible the children should learn. The peasants really got along not bad with us but they were poisoned by the church. They made pogroms. In the middle of the night they could get up and go into Jewish houses and kill for no reason whatsoever and the government turned a blind eye to it. What could you do when you were not prepared? It didn't happen every day, you didn't know when it's going to bust out. How could you be prepared when somebody came at night and knocked your windows out? What could you do?

It is, I suppose, too extreme to accuse a whole nation. With the Poles, I follow what Abraham said to God: "If in Sodom and Gomorrah will be ten good people, would you destroy the whole city?" God tells him no. "If there is three good people there would you destroy it?" God says no. "If there is one human being, a good man, in Sodom and Gomorrah, would you destroy the whole city?" God said, "No." God destroyed the city, so that means there was not even one good man. I cannot say that about the Poles.

Every human being is an animal, just let him free to do everything he wants and it could happen here too what happened in Europe. I believe that. Any people ripe for it. It's not such an extraordinary idea. Just look what people did to other people over the last two thousand years.

My whole life was one single desire: to get out of Poland. I wanted to go even by foot. Everyone of us had that dream but we had no ways and means to do so, we didn't have the money and nobody wanted to leave the parents, we were too young. The dream was, "If I grow up, I'll go to the United States, or Paris, or wherever, just out of Poland." We couldn't take the difference between a Jew and a non-Jew. I couldn't stand the hate. My father was always dreaming of Israel, but he couldn't afford it, we were nine kids. And the worst thing that broke him physically and mentally was when the store was robbed because we had to work and work just to be able to eat, not to dress, just to eat. Everybody wanted to go to Israel, and there were organizations that helped, but not with money. I think it was over a thousand dollars you needed and that was not so easy. My father, if he had the money for Israel, he would go blindly. I thought a lot about it too, I was a Zionist but not an official party man. I never belonged officially to any party. But there's no question about it, I felt the Jews' natural place was in Israel. Besides, it wasn't a matter only of money, you had to have papers to go to Israel and England didn't let you in. You had to go through a lot, but oh, we would have done anything to get out of Poland.

First, I wanted to go to Paris because I had some friends who were studying medicine there and they wrote me how nice it was. My friends and me, we were very anxious to know how it is in America. We didn't know very much about it but we did know there's more freedom there, that anti-Semitism is less. I remember a man came to visit from the United States, his parents lived in Pinczow. When he stepped off the train, people were running to meet him — everybody wanted to see what a Jew from America looked like. He said, "I was sitting on the train and saw what's going on here." He had on his lapel a pin that he's an American. "I took it off and kissed it and put it back tightly on my lapel." That was for us an amazing thing to witness.

Wherever you went, whatever you did to get away from prejudice, from fear, a brick wall was in front of you.

Just a year before the war, I read in the newspaper that they were auditioning actors in Warsaw for a film. I told my father that I'm going to work in Warsaw, I would get a better job there. I had to lie. It wasn't such a big lie. First of all, I did work as a knitter in Warsaw because I knew the wages were much higher there than in Lodz. But at the same time I thought about getting into films. It was very, very hard for Jews to get work because they were saying we were taking jobs away from the Poles. But I was a dreamer and I went to Warsaw to audition. They listened to me, and when I told them my name, Israel Rubinek, they looked at me and right away said, "We will let you know." They were anti-Semitic but more sophisticated, they didn't stop me from auditioning, that wouldn't have been polite. There was also another film about a cabaret and they needed actors who knew how to dance. I showed them what I could do but the director told me he couldn't let me do the job. I danced very well but I was too small for the girl. I was in Warsaw for about a half a year working in a factory. I didn't get any acting jobs, then the factory work stopped because there was a slack period and I had to come back to Lodz.

I was thinking a lot about theatre. I loved to create, I enjoyed every minute of it. And I gave it up because there was no way, no means to do something about it. It was just a dream. There was not time enough, the war broke off everything, the whole life broke off.

Part Two

Nineteen thirty-nine, in August I turned nineteen, then two weeks later the war broke out. We heard on the radio that the Poles lost right away, I think after two days or so, and the Germans are coming. We were so frightened, we heard what was going on in the thirties in Germany, the Jews were running out since 1933. What do you think, we didn't know? We knew enough to be afraid.

My father had a policy that we should not stay together: together we're going to die together. He was right. After just one day or two, he sent my oldest brothers, Srulcie and Chamel, to run away to Lublin to be with my grandfather.

The rest of us took all the shoes in stock from the store down to the basement and we hid there too, figuring, firstly, if we have all the shoes we'll be able to live on something, and secondly, if there's fire the basement will be safe and maybe the Germans won't find us.

They came after three days, they came. We were sitting there in that basement and we could hear German being yelled on the street: "*Komme raus!*" Come out! Oh, I'll never forget it. And we could see smoke is coming into the basement, the house upstairs is burning already and we were choking. Then we heard loud: "*Komme raus! Komme raus!*" from the top of the stairs but they didn't come down, afraid somebody could shoot from the basement. So we had no choice. There was a little kerosene lamp, my father closed it so there shouldn't be fire in that full basement of shoes, and we went up, what could we do, with our hands in the air, and they ran us to the church on the corner of the square. All the Jews they took out and all the houses all around the square were burning when I was running, and they were chasing us to that churchyard and put machine-guns all around and they were shooting at us too, even with the children there. Just shooting, just for fun, and who caught the bullet was dead, I was too scared to even look around, everybody was yelling, one on top of the other like hay falling. I was so young, people were killed right beside me, and when did I ever see something before like this, never in my life. My father said, "That's it! Now they're going to shoot us all!" He said, "Let's run to the wall! Let's be the first one at the wall!" And we ran! We ran fast to the wall of the church, by a big door. In a second there was a mountain of people there, and they were shooting, and shooting! And screaming! The screams! I can still hear the screams. And then after a half an hour, they stopped. And when they stopped, and it was quiet, I got up slowly, and I said, "My God! We are all alive? This was a miracle! So many bodies here, and we're still alive here? This is a miracle, we're still alive." We were in that yard for three days and two nights and then they chased all of us out, didn't watch us any more, and they didn't care suddenly where we went.

The house was burned, everything was a ruin. We went to the flour mill and stayed there, eight of us: my parents, my mother's parents, my two sisters and me, and Yossele. I wanted to be in Lublin with my older brothers. My father gave permission but he wouldn't let me travel alone. I went with a very nice boy from a very Chassidic family, but he himself was already a little bit more modern. He was the same age as me and yet Father let me go. You know, we slept in the same room, that boy was such a gentleman, I just can't tell you, from a very good family.

Well, it was very hard to travel because the trains weren't yet functioning properly, so we went by horse and wagon, by train, lifts, whatever. When we arrived at my grandfather's house it was all closed up. He had there a business together with the house, wholesale textiles, trimmings, and linings for men's hats. Nobody was there.

My aunt Topcie and her husband lived in Lublin. We went to their house and there was Grandfather, afraid to stay in his own house because it was in the business section of the city.

Also staying with Topcie was another aunt of mine, Sarah, but she was only a few months older than me. My brothers were gone. They told me that after only a few days in Lublin, Chamel and Srulcie ran away to Russia.

The Germans were in Lublin everywhere, soldiers and guns. People were staying in their houses and walking faster on the street. One day, things were a little quieter, more back to normal, my grandfather said Sarah and I should go to his textile business to bring something back, I forget what it was. We went, and as soon as we opened the store, a man followed us in right away and started to take merchandise. We could see right away that this man was a *Volksdeutsche*. You know what this is? A German living as Polish citizen in Poland but collaborating with the Germans: "fifth columnist" they call it. We could recognize them right away. He just took whatever he wanted without paying, like it's his right. We were too frightened to make trouble. Well, he left, and we were just recovering from this, in comes two SS officers. Do we live here? No. Where? We had to give Topcie's address. They yelled at us for a while, who remembers what, and then they started to pick merchandise for themselves, also for no money, just picked. Did anybody else take out merchandise from the store, they wanted to know. So we told them about the *Volksdeutsche* who came before them and took. Well, this made them mad, they were SS and had the right to take but nobody else did. Could we recognize him? Yes. Something will be done. Meanwhile they made a parcel of what merchandise they liked and said we have to come to such and such address tonight to bring them this parcel, me and Sarah. Can you imagine how much aggravation this was? Not to go, we were afraid. To go, we were even more afraid.

Anyway, nine o'clock that night, we took that parcel, me and Sarah, and went to the address they gave us. It was a house where a Polish family probably used to live but the SS used to kick the people out and take it over for themselves. We came in, gave them the material and you know, we were lucky that time to get out of there alive. They let us stand a little bit there in that room, we were still terrified. A dog was there that looked three times as big as me. They looked at us, looked at us and then one comes over to me, quietly: "If I want, you would now undress and dance naked on that table for me." I didn't say a word, I was just standing there like a fool. We stood a little longer and then they let us go, just like that.

A few days later two German officers, different ones, came to Topje's house and asked me questions about that *Volksdeutsche* that stole merchandise. But I knew I would be afraid to point a finger if I saw that man: he could come next day and kill me. The officers were very polite, explaining about order and right, and we were there, Grandfather, Topje, Sarah and me, all of us shaking. They took me out to their car and drove me around the whole day to different villages around Lublin to find that *Volksdeutsche*, to recognize him. The SS officers talked to me, they were very nice, my God, they even bought me lunch. Finally we came to a place and I saw him, believe me, he turned white when he saw it's me, but I said no, I don't recognize him. Are you sure? Sure I'm sure, I saw him, how can I not recognize him? I didn't hear from him again but if I would have said yes, I would have heard, don't worry.

I stayed in Lublin four weeks, I missed my family and went back to Pinczow, again travelling with that very nice boy.

⤳ *ISRAEL* ⤶

Nineteen thirty-nine, in the spring before the war, I was working in a Lodz factory as a mechanic of knitting machines. One day a German worker, Herr Bittner was his name, a nice quiet man, came to me and begged me to do something he shouldn't be fired, he has three children at home. You see, Lodz was a city with many people of German descent, *Volksdeutsche*, and before the war the Poles were sure Hitler will invade Poland, so from fear of spies they started to throw out all the Germans working in their factories. I went to the boss and told him Bittner was a good man, his children wouldn't have what to eat if he threw him out. He said, you take the responsibility and I said all right. Later on, the factory had a money shortage, the boss fired me, and Herr Bittner was still working there.

I know now that many of these *Volksdeutsche* in fact were spies. September 1st, 1939, Hitler invaded Poland. We had a neighbour on our steet, Narutowitce Street, a very polite German, and when the Nazi bombers started to fly over our heads, from down on the street we saw that German on the roof with a swastika flag, making signs to the planes. He was scared because the Poles could kill him but he was living among Jews, and only Jews saw him do it, Jews too scared to do or say anything.

People were running on the streets, it was chaos. The Polish police asked everyone to go down to their cellars. It was a peculiar thing, we didn't know personally very much about our neighbours when we were living there in the same building, but in the cellar, that day, we met them, after sitting there all day and all night while the bombers were flying. When it was quiet, people started to talk to each other, not so afraid any more, and a man came up to me, introduced himself and asked me what kind of work I do. When I told him I'm a very good mechanic of knitting machines, he grabbed his head and said he had one of the biggest factories in Lodz of shoelaces, and he couldn't get a good mechanic. So if he would have known about me before, I could have made with him not less than two hundred zlotys a week all year round. I was so stunned, I was looking for work all the time when it was slack, and I didn't know that next to me my neighbour could have given me such a good living.

The Germans did two things to panic the people: first of all, a few months before the war, they took in all the change money, coins — there were German banks in Poland and they made sure there was a shortage. Nobody could go out with five zlotys paper bill to buy something and get change. That the Germans did for sure, made chaos. They also did another thing: a rumour came that the first thing the Nazis will do when they come is kill the Jewish youth. My father said, "I cannot conceive that people will come in and just kill for nothing." He never believed it.

But when the Nazis started marching into Poland, we didn't know if it's better to run or to stay. My friend Itche Kashteinski wanted to run to Warsaw, maybe it will be easier for Jews in a bigger city. I wanted to go. My father said he could not run suddenly with seven small kids to Warsaw. My older brother Chaim-David was too weak, too much a dreamer to run. My father said to me, "Go and let God bless you."

We started walking to Warsaw, Itche Kashteinski and me. On the way were thousands of people, Jews, Poles, walking, in carriages, on wagons, horses, with parcels, carpets, whatever they couldn't physically carry out from their house, they left behind. I saw, I still remember, a beautiful motorcycle, left behind — no gas. We went into houses for a drop of water on the way, into empty villages, farmers were running away, we saw even meals on the table untouched.

Warsaw was already surrounded and the German army was going by tanks, trucks, and motorcycles, on the road to Lodz, thousands of them.

We were walking on a field, a group of ten of us, the road was just a few yards away, and suddenly a bunch of motorcycles stopped, looked at us, then came and surrounded us. What's your name, what's your name, you, and you! People told their name and were let go. They came to me, I said, "Israel Rubinek." They looked at me and started to yell, "A Polish Jew?" I said, "Yes." They called all around for the soldiers to come look at me, they caught a Polish Jew. They stared at me like I would have some horns on my head, they didn't want to touch me, just walked around like hundreds of years ago the Indians were dancing around a fire, everybody asking, "Polish Jew?" "Polish Jew?" When they got tired of it, they left on their motorcycles, without hurting us.

We were walking for two days. At night was not too bad, but in the daytime the airplanes came down shooting the people like cows. I saw people falling dead near me, I was running, behind me they were falling but the bullets didn't catch me.

The Germans later waited till hundreds of us accumulated, surrounded us with motorcycles and pushed us into an open field. It didn't matter if you were a Pole or a Jew, everybody was scared of them. Right away with the Germans has to be order: they told us to sit down, all of us, with hands behind the head. We were sitting like this for hours, and the sun was just cooking. Then, one by one, we were called and they asked, "Jew, or not Jew?" It just came into my mind when it was my turn to say, "No." And my friend Itche said also, "No." All who said yes, they put later on trucks and who knows but I think they took them right away to Germany for labour. The rest of us they let go.

You see, every single Jew in Europe, you recognized in the eyes. In Europe you knew it was a Jew even if he was blond with a small nose. The eyes. When I came to Canada, I was watching the boys when they came out of that club, the YMHA, and I said, "They're not Jews." The eyes were free. You know the difference? In Europe, the eyes told you, "I am afraid."

Recently I met in Miami a man, he was eighty-three years old, tall, walked straight, red hair, he was a fireman from Michigan. Did I get shocked. One morning he took off the shirt for swimming and I see he's wearing a Star of David around his neck. He was a Jew! I would never guess in a million years. He was an American-born Jew and I felt from him the same freedom I felt in the eyes of the boys from the YMHA. It's true, I find the same thing with many Jews in America but not so much as with that fireman. Some Jews, even born here, you can tell they're mixing in a little bit in their talk a Yiddish tune. But that man — absolute, nothing. He carried himself like a non-Jew, talked like a non-Jew, he never talked about Jewishness. Just normally an absolute American. It just happens he was born a Jew, that's all. I saw nothing he's ashamed of and I was jealous, that he has no worries. He was proud of Judaism. That was nice. He didn't know a thing about it but he was proud of it: "I don't care, I'd stand up for anybody." I was looking at him with amazement, with jealousy. How can a man not be scared of anything? His face was so — "I am!"

The truth is at the beginning of the war the Germans could not differentiate who is a Jew and who not because I saw them ask even a Chassidic man with a beard and sidecurls if he's Jewish. They didn't know if we had a specific face or something, not yet, but the Poles knew us and the Poles turned on us, like we knew they would.

We went back on the road but we couldn't keep walking into the German army straight in the face. The heart went out of us, we turned around and went in the same direction as the soldiers, back to Lodz.

FRANIA

My grandparents' beautiful house was on the same square as ours and it burned right to the ground. A few months before the war, they were the richest in town and now overnight they had nothing. But the Germans didn't take away their flour mill yet — it wasn't working but it was a place for us to live. It was a little outside of town and on the same property was a little caretaker's house, two rooms and a kitchen, that's all, for eight of us.

In the town the Jews were allowed to walk only on sidestreets not on main streets. Also another law: we had to wear armbands with a yellow Star of David.

Around that time my two sisters and me and Yossele started to sneak on the sidestreets of Pinczow, one of us was always running in front to see if the Germans were passing, then we were hiding in burned homes until we got to our burned house on the square and into the basement. We had hundreds of shoes there, you understand, we wanted to smuggle them back to the mill, they were worth a lot of money. The shoes were all in boxes, everything covered in dirt and smoke from the fire so when we came out of there we looked like coalminers. We took the shoes out of the boxes, put them into big bags and like this we carried them back to the mill. Imagine, we smuggled like this every day, twice a day, for two weeks and it was from Pinczow to the mill like from my house now to the Westgate Shopping Centre — maybe three miles. I don't know how I did it, by nerves I suppose. But we had something to sell and something to live on.

By the mill, near us, lived a man with his wife in a small house. He saw how we were making a living on those shoes, he got jealous and he squealed on us. One night, just after supper, two German soldiers came in and said we have to give them the shoes. Well, what can you do? Right away they'll start to threaten with guns so we started bringing out bags of shoes. While we were doing this one of the soldiers — oh! a face like a murderer, I'll never forget it — started to stare at me and I knew what he was getting at. He didn't do anything yet, scared I guess. You know they were not allowed by Nazi racial law to sleep with Jewish women, "*Rassenschande*" it was called, we weren't good enough to rape. He kept staring at me, I was so frightened, I saw it was eating him up, the frustration. Suddenly, he grabbed my father and went outside and just to bother him, aggravate, scare him, he started ordering my father to run! lie down! run! lie down! and it was October — muddy, cold, very wet — and my father had a weak heart, he couldn't stand up

any more. Finally he dragged my father inside and started to
come right for me, he was hot already, he worked himself up to
it. My mother is sitting there, the whole family standing there
— it didn't matter to him, he's coming right to me. I got so
frightened, I was sure he was going to rape me right there, my
blood went cold and I fainted. The other soldier, when he saw
this, he started to yell at his partner that it was not allowed and
he took out his gun and said he'll shoot him if he goes further.
So the other one backed off, they grabbed the bags of shoes and
ran away.

They thought they confiscated everything but half the bags
of shoes we had hidden in another place so we still had half to
live on.

The flour mill began to operate once again, controlled by the
Germans through an overseer. You've never seen such a gentle
man, in his seventies already, from the old Germans, aristo-
cratic. It happened that he came by the next day and saw that
my father is so sick, he asked what was the matter. My father
told him the story, everything in detail. The old man said he's
going to look into this — would I recognize that soldier? Oh
yes, I can't forget him. Well, he found him, the old man, and he
called me to identify him. Yes, that's the man. I don't know
what they did to him, but they fixed him up, don't worry. I had
my revenge. From that incident my father became very sick
and it lasted a long time, his heart was bad.

∞ *ISRAEL* ∞

At home in Lodz, everybody was scared to go out, every day we
heard that somebody we knew was shot, every day they
published new laws against us: a Jew can't intermarry with
Gentiles, or work at certain kinds of business, or go here, or

walk there. Later came the order that Jews had to make themselves a Star of David armband.

In those days there were long line-ups for bread in our city. You could wait in line all day for one loaf. One day I went out early to buy bread for the family and on the street German soldiers grabbed me and took me with a bunch of other people to a train station that they made into a big warehouse where I saw there were hundreds of people working. I saw thousands of kerchiefs, all kinds and colours, everybody standing at tables to put those kerchiefs straight and wrap them in packages for shipment to Germany. So I was standing there working all day long. It was also a little comical. For a long time they forgot to give me boxes to put the kerchiefs in so I kept piling them higher and higher on the table until I couldn't reach. I was scared to ask for boxes so I looked around, I didn't see Gestapo watching, I pulled the pile down and started again. Most of the day — piled it up, tore it down and started again. A man came around later with boxes and I stood there all day long with nothing to eat till six o'clock. Then they threw us out, told us to go home. I saw a soldier sitting, counting everyone who went out. I thought to myself: I'm going to ask, he can say no, I have nothing to lose. I came up to the soldier and said politely, in German, "I would like to have a statement signed that I worked all day and authorization to buy bread without lining up." I remember that German was not a Gestapo, he was from the Wehrmacht, the regular army. He wore glasses, he looked at me curiously for a moment, thought about it and said, "You know what? You're quite right." He made out the authorization for me. I was probably the only one who asked for it.

When I got home that day, everybody was waiting to see if I'll come home alive. In the morning, I went out very early, before the curfew allowed. You see, I went out always without the Star of David armband because even though the Poles were under curfew too, they were allowed out three hours earlier than the Jews and whenever a Jew came to a bread line-up it was already four, five blocks long.

Every line-up had soldiers watching that it ran in order, straight. I took my paper with the authorization, went up to a soldier and showed it to him. And you know, he pushed away everybody else and I was the first to get bread. I ran home fast. But mine was a big family, lots of kids, all hungry. So I started thinking, if it worked once, why shouldn't I try it in other places? Lodz is a big city. I ran around that day to quite a few line-ups and every soldier, when I showed him my paper, took me to the front of the line. I brought home four, five loaves and that was worth more than gold — gold you couldn't eat.

The authorization was dated for one day only but I carefully erased it and every day I marked a new date, for almost two weeks, until my piece of paper just finally wore out.

Then I was like everybody else. Again I would go out earlier than Jews were allowed, without my armband, to get bread for the family. It so happened that one morning I ran into Herr Bittner, the German who used to work with me in the factory, the man whose job I saved. Herr Bittner was now in the uniform of the Gestapo. He saw I'm not wearing the Star of David and he started screaming at me that he doesn't know me any more, times have changed, I'm breaking the law, better run away or he'll shoot me right where I stand. I was astonished, shocked. I stood there probably with open mouth. A man that I gave to eat, a man that I helped — if my boss would have squealed on me that I stood up for a *Volksdeutsche* to work in the factory, the Poles could have jailed me as a spy — now Herr Bittner sees me without an armband and he's ready to kill me. That's the German personality for you — I believe that every nation has its peculiarities — as for the German, either he's on top of you, or he's under you. If under you, he's like a dog, wiggles his tail, and he's ready to shine your shoes. But when he's on top of you, he's the master of you and at your throat.

A few days later, I again went out before curfew allowed,

without the armband, around four o'clock in the morning — even before the Poles were allowed out. There were a few of us hiding near a wall, waiting to be the first in the line-up for bread. Gestapo caught us. There were seven of us, all Poles, nobody knew I'm a Jew. We didn't have time even to think, it was a sudden thing — "Hands up! Face the wall!" I didn't know what will happen, I just stood there, I was the first one in line on the left side, looking at the wall, my hands up. It was so fast, I didn't even feel what happened, I just heard a bang and the woman next to me fell down dead, that's all, and another bang, and one more — every second person shot straight in the head. I didn't have the nerve even to turn my head to look, I thought I'm next. Suddenly they yelled "*Los! los! los!*" Run! Run! So the three of us who were left alive started to run, I didn't look where I was going, just ran. I found myself in a doorway to a courtyard, I went in, sat down on the ground and just breathed. I couldn't come to myself, I was shivering, in shock, couldn't really grasp in my brain what had happened to me and I sat there till the night was over and I came to my senses. I walked home. The war was already a few months old but it had not till then come so close to me, right beside me.

One thing I knew — I wanted to get out of Lodz. You can imagine, that shooting at the wall just sat in my brain and now that I was scared to break curfew for bread we all went a little more hungry than normal — and normal was already bitter.

One day my father came home and said that he saw a young Jewish boy begging in the street, begging for a piece of bread, anything — and that boy looked familiar but he didn't know who it was. Well, it was my brother, Yitzchak. Later Yitzchak came in and my father realized it was his son who was the beggar and he started to cry, he just couldn't conceive that he walked by and didn't recognize his own son. He cried probably half a day.

I just couldn't take the pain, to see the kids hungry, crying. Wherever you looked in our house was someone else crying,

crying. It made my father helpless, it was impossible to do anything about it, it took the life out of me and I just knew I must leave, I must go "home," to Pinczow. We heard that Pinczow was burned but we didn't know who was alive and who not — and the truth is I was also thinking of Frania.

It wasn't one thing specifically that pushed me to leave Lodz — in the first place, I thought I will be able to come back — it was everything together. Finally, what decided me, though, was the forced work order. You see, the Germans very quickly set up a council of Jewish elders, a *Judenrat*, who passed on to the rest of us the Nazi orders. The *Judenrat* sent out lists of Jewish youth who had to report for work, labour for the Germans and when I saw my name there I decided that I'm not going to do it. Why? The incident with Herr Bittner made a scary impression on me — Lodz was a city with many German nationals like him and I felt that in such a large city if we went to labour for them, they could do with us what they wanted, we might not come home at the end of the day.

I decided to leave. My father didn't want me to, all the kids liked me very much, they were hanging on my legs — but I couldn't help it, I said I'm going, I'm taking off the armband, my face is not typically Jewish, I speak a good Polish, a good German and I'm going to see if maybe in Pinczow I can do something to help. I'll be back.

My father walked down with me into the yard. My father was not an emotional man — he was a good man but he kept his feelings buried inside — I hardly ever saw him cry — only on Yom Kippur in the synagogue, one day a year, he would weep so powerfully his whole body shook from it — but that day, in the yard before I left, I looked at him, I was shocked, I wasn't expecting it, tears were pouring from his eyes like blood.

"I won't see you again," he said.

He could barely talk, tears were running in his beard, he put his hand on my head and blessed me. So I started to cry too and he put his arms around me and squeezed me and said, "May God save you and protect you from evil."

I was numb, I walked out the gate into the street, and later when I looked back he was still standing there in the yard, crying.

I walked 250 kilometres to Pinczow. Four days. On the way I passed through the small town of Pietrkow and standing there in the middle of the way was a whole bunch of Gestapo. I wasn't alone, a lot of people were walking, but I didn't know who was a Jew and who was not, because nobody was asking questions. The Gestapo was stopping everybody — looking, asking, letting some go, some not. I saw also a lot of *Volksdeutsche* that just went by and said, "Heil Hitler," and they let them go, no questions. Well, you know I was an actor, so when it came to me, I went by with my parcel saying "HEIL HITLER!" So they didn't look at me, just let me pass.

I came to Pinczow, I met a whole picture. My aunts, my uncle, my grandmother, in a hole. They had a house before, a store — everything burned down to nothing. They were all sitting in a small room, nothing to eat, crying.

Grandmother was there. My aunt Surele was there with her husband and two small children, and her younger sister, my aunt Hadas. My grandfather died a few years before, he was the lucky one — he was dead for normal reasons.

The life was terrible. There were restricted places in Pinczow where a Jew couldn't walk even — if he was walking, they were shooting him. We were treated like dogs. Worse than dogs: a dog could go, but we couldn't go.

After a while my grandmother rented a small, very small store. Just to make a living. Bread and coffee, that's all you could buy there. I had a few zlotys, I bought a bike, and I rode back on the bike to Lodz — as a Pole, not as a Jew. My plan was to buy merchandise for the store because they couldn't get it somewhere else. By the time I came back to Pinczow after a few days, my behind was with blisters from the bicycle. That I could never forget. It was raining on the way and I had on my shoulders a sack, between my legs another sack, and I was riding hard, I didn't want to stop. For a whole week I had to lay down, I couldn't sit. Whenever I went with the bike I came back always very sick, exhausted. But I didn't know another way to help out.

When I was in Lodz, of course I saw my family. Everybody was wearing the blue Star of David on a white background. Not on the arm but on their front lapel and on the backs too. So you could see if it's a Jew from behind or in front. That was the law. You had to do it or right away be killed. I told my father I'll go back and forth another few times, maybe I can help, bring things or even take the family to Pinczow. But I only went like this with the bicycle twice before they created the ghetto in Lodz and I couldn't get through any more.

It's funny, when I first went walking to Pinczow that time when I took off the armband and my father stood crying, that's when I thought maybe I'll never see him and the kids again. But I did — twice more when I came back on the bicycle. And when I really was seeing them all for the last time, I left with no special feeling — I thought I'll be back soon.

Half a year later a Polish friend told me he is going to Lodz, so I said I want to go with him. It was winter and we went in a sleigh. We made holes in the sleigh to hide small money. Eighteen kilometres before Lodz we came to the border. There was a new German border outside the city because, by this time, Lodz was connected to the German Reich — they made Lodz "Litzmannstadt." So at the border the Gestapo kept everybody — asking, asking — and to me they said they don't believe I'm a Pole. They let the other people go, including my friend with the sleigh, and they dragged me into the office. The Gestapo beat me and yelled at me to take off the pants, to take off everything: he wants to see if I am a Jew or not. I hesitated. I took it very slow, because I knew it's going to be the end of me. Suddenly came in a higher rank of Gestapo, and asked what is going on. They told him. He looked at me and he said, "Is he a Jew, or not a Jew, the hell with him, throw him out." They threw me out half naked.

I walked back forty kilometres to Pietrkow and it was twenty-five below zero. When I got there I was almost frozen to death. Finally, I got a train towards Pinczow. I acted like a drunk Polish peasant — I put up my feet and pretended to sleep. Soon two Gestapo came into the train car, pushed my feet off the seat and sat down right in front of me. I kept my eyes closed, I snored a little bit. A few kilometres later, the train stopped, a few Gestapo came in with maybe ten, fifteen Jews as prisoners. One of those Jews — he was in bad shape, who knows what they did to him — was somebody I knew, I used to be in school with him. He looked at me, stared at me. Suddenly he started to yell — in Yiddish: "Israel! You know me. Help me! Tell my parents I'm arrested by Gestapo!" He didn't realize probably what he's doing, he was in panic. Everybody looked at me — I wasn't wearing an armband. I yelled at my friend in Polish: "I don't know you, and you don't know me! I am not a Jew!" But the Poles on the side started to look at me up and down. They said, "You know, you look like a Jew." I swore at them, I told them that probably they are Jews themselves. And like a Polish peasant every second word I said was "Jesus Christ" or "Jesus Maria." When I start to raise my voice, they settled down, because I was too sure of myself to be a Jew.

❦ FRANIA ❧

By springtime of '40 we had a little money already from selling those shoes that we smuggled, and the flour mill brought in something too. We figured we'll try to build up our house that was burned. So my brother Yossele was the one who supervised it. He really worked hard because the other two brothers weren't at home, they were in Russia — who knew if they're even alive.

We moved back in the house, my parents, grandparents, sisters, and brother, in the fall of '40, so we were in the flour mill for twelve months or so. The store was still burned in front and we left it that way, but in the back we built everything new. You know when you build, you can make a place where to hide things. We still had left some soft leather to make shoes, and this was worth a lot of money. Some Poles helped us with the construction — we thought we could trust them. Well, one day came the Germans, with a truck, they went right to that hiding place, and they took everything, but everything.

I don't know, I wouldn't say that the Gentiles did it. You think there weren't Jews who gave one another away? If they saw that you have something to eat, the jealousy ate them. Listen, that's war: some people are nice, and some people are showing they are just like animals.

So I don't know who or how, but the Germans came one day and took out everything — they cleaned us out so that we didn't have next day even a bread to buy. So the bakery shop there, listen, they knew us, that we were such a respected family. My father said I should go for two breads in the morning, and I said, "I'm not going for the bread. How are you going to have money to pay? I'm not going." And I didn't. My father had to go by himself, I was too embarrassed.

Every single day, we ate black bread — every single day, three times a day. We had a lot of potatoes, so my mother cooked a potato soup, and we had that with bread and butter. Three times a day we ate this. Believe me, compared to later, life was sugar-sweet.

In the meantime, you know, I was going out with Israel. He lived with his grandmother there, but he didn't come to my house, I didn't dare ask him. He never came inside the mill when we were living there either. My parents knew that I'm going with him, and they didn't like it but I saw him anyway — I couldn't help it.

His grandmother had a little grocery store. He was working there, helping out, sitting there all the time in that store, so I used to go and the whole day I was sitting there too. Or we saw each other on the street. We were walking the sidestreets, you know, just like thieves we were going.

When the Germans came in, a lot of Jews were running for their life to Russia. So Israel said, "Now it's a good time, we could get away, everybody's going, we could smuggle into Russia."

"Not me. I wouldn't do it. My conscience, I wouldn't be able to live with. I'd give up my marriage, I wouldn't do it. I'll never do this to hurt my father." It's funny — I didn't say "mother," but I said "my father."

He said, "But you're going to save your life. What's going to happen to us in Poland? Now we're young, we could go."

"I'm not running away. They're going to say Shloime Baruch's daughter ran off with a boy. I would never do this to hurt my father. *Qué sera, sera,* — what's going to be will be, but if I'm meant to be alive, I'll live — and we'll get married too." But when was that going to happen? I figured we're going to go together so long, till my parents will say "It's enough already." And that's what happened.

That summer while the house was being rebuilt, my brother Chamel came back from Russia — without Srulcie, my oldest brother. Chamel left him there and came back himself because Srulcie wanted to stay. And probably when he did want to come back, it was already too late. Maybe they caught him on the border in Russia and said that he is a spy — the Russians did that to a lot of Jews. But really who knows what happened? I don't know, maybe they sent him to Siberia. He was a very delicate boy, probably died from the hard work in the woods and everything. Who knows? We never found out about him. Never.

Chamel came back and went to Lublin. He was working for a German factory, made a lot of money there, sent quite a bit to us. You know, he was so intelligent, I told you, he had such a terrific head on his shoulders. He was doing bookkeeping, he had forty shoemakers there sitting making shoes, and he was the whole manager of this, you understand. Let's say, when a transport of leather came, right away he sold it to somebody on the black market. The Germans didn't know anything – that's why he had so much money. He would always send money to us with Gentile couriers. No matter how the times got hard, Chamel always found a way to send money for us. And that's the way we lived. What did we do? Nothing, we lived, we were just frightened, that's all. Just every day, from day to day we were waiting for the Messiah to come.

My brother Chamel wrote letters from Lublin, saying he wants to take us out, get us to Lublin where he could help us better. But we didn't know things were going to happen so fast, that soon the Germans would take out all the Jews to the concentration camps. And we didn't believe it, either. Once a man came into town yelling that he ran away from a concentration camp, that all the Jews were taken out of his town, deported to a camp. He told the story, he swore the Nazis burned people, killed them. Nobody believed him. What's he talking? He's nuts.

So at the beginning, we didn't know what's going on. We thought, yes, they take all these Jews to heavy labour, but to kill? We couldn't even realize what was happening. I don't remember talking this over with Israel at all. I knew one thing: I wanted to get married, that's all, that's all I knew.

❦ ISRAEL ❧

Every day the *Judenrat* in Pinczow had to give a contingent of people to the Germans for work – digging, fixing railroads.

I got up in the morning, we opened my grandmother's store, sometimes the *Judenrat* sent me to work. I had to go, my name was on the list. If not, you couldn't go out, they caught you on the street, and took you to work. The Germans would take a bunch of us first to one place for labour, then another place, and so on. I always stayed the last one in the group and when it got a little bit darker, I slowed down. As I was at the end of the line, and because I am a small size, I could sneak away and run home. You see, we never knew what they'll do to us at the end of a day. I got scared I'm never coming home again. I could have got shot, but I was trying always to run away.

The marketplace in Pinczow was probably a quarter of a kilometre around, and in the middle was a park. One day, I was walking across the middle of the market. On the left side of me, in a corner, was standing a Gestapo. He yelled at me — he wants me to come. I saw him right away when I was walking, but he didn't see that I see him. If I would run away, he would shoot after me, so I pretended I don't see him. He was on the left side of me, and he was yelling, so I was looking on the right side. And walking. He yelled and yelled his head off, and I looked all over, like "Where is this voice coming from?" I turned my head, in the back, in the front, and the right side, never on his side. The more he was screaming, the more I was turning my head, like I would hear an echo from the other side. And walking, and walking. When I came to the corner, at a burned house, I started to run. And he start to run after me. But I went in the burned house, between the stones, and I lay down there all day long — he was looking for me, but he couldn't find me. And at night-time I went home.

Another incident: I was coming home from my friend — his name was Shmulek Finer, he's still alive in Warsaw, now. There was in Pinczow one Gestapo man, he couldn't eat breakfast, or lunch, or supper, without shooting somebody. Before he went to eat he would shoot a few people in the street. When they saw him in the street, everybody was running home. When I was walking home from my friend, I heard from behind me: "*Stehen bleiben!*" Stop! There were empty houses near, so I just walked in one, went behind the door, and stood there. He came after me. Found me right away.

"Why did you run away?"

I told him, "I didn't run away, I walked away."

He asked me, "Why you're staying here in the corner hidden?"

I said, "I have to go to the bathroom and I haven't got where. So I'm staying in the corner and I'm doing my human things."

He gave me a slap in the face, and walked away. That was the same son of a gun who killed people all the time, like nothing. Why not me? Ask him.

One time I was coming home from a date with Frania. The curfew was seven o'clock — I came home two minutes past. Right at my door a Gestapo caught me.

"Why are you on the street?"

I said, "I am not on the street, I am before my house."

"Why did you go out?"

"Because the toilet is outside."

He said, "You're lying." And he started to hit me.

Across us was living a man named Kopecz, the Captain of the Polish police, and some other Poles — we were living among the Poles — and they came running to watch. Like a sport. Anyway, the Gestapo was hitting me with his closed hand. They were usually used to Jews begging them to leave them alone, offering money, rings, anything. The Poles were yelling to me, "Rubinek! Beg him!" They were yelling and laughing, "Beg him and maybe he won't kill you." I didn't say a single word — I just looked at the Gestapo, plain in the eyes. So he took out his revolver and hit me over the head. I fell down. Kopecz the policeman said, "Soon there will be a Jew less." He was laughing his head off. Well, after banging me on the head for a while, maybe the Gestapo got bored with it — I wasn't begging or crying or screaming — anyway, he finally let me go inside.

My grandmother and aunt were watching from the window,

terrified. They washed me, I fainted. It didn't take ten minutes, the Gestapo came to the house and called me out. He asked me if I speak German. I said, yes, I speak German. It's a peculiar thing: when he was hitting, he was yelling like a pig, but when he needed me, he talked politely. He wanted me to be the translator to a Pole, the Pole doesn't understand German. I said, okay, I'll do it.

Sure enough, he took me into that Captain Kopecz's office across the street. He told me to tell the Pole that he wants to take the desk there for his own office — the police captain should give it to him. I was thinking fast, that it was my opportunity — that I'm going to laugh, before my death, I'm going to laugh a little bit. And have revenge.

I told Kopecz what the Gestapo said.

Kopecz said, "Let him take it."

I told the Gestapo, "He doesn't want to give it."

The Gestapo gave him a slap in the face.

I said to Kopecz, "Beg him. Maybe he won't kill you." So Kopecz started to beg *me* to tell the Gestapo he could take the desk — he plain went on his knees to me, to beg him.

So I said, "I'll beg him." I said, "He's begging you shouldn't take the desk."

The Gestapo hit him so much, that a little bit of revenge I got. Before he was laughing at me bleeding and now I was laughing ten minutes later — nobody knows whose tomorrow it is. Well, he begged me and begged me, and the truth is I couldn't look how he was hit, so I told the Gestapo, "You don't have to ask him favours. You are the law here — take it." And that's what he did — took the table, and went away.

Kopecz didn't know what happened. He thought I saved his life.

We didn't know what the Germans plans were. We were guessing but we were not sure. We knew that they were killing Jews — in Pinczow and Lodz I saw killing — but we didn't think that there's such a thing as Auschwitz, Majdanek, anything like that, that there's special organized places, that they're gathering the Jews, and killing.

There was an incident: to the rabbi of Pinczow came two Jews and told him that they ran away from a concentration camp called Treblinka. They were working in Treblinka to sort out the clothes from the dead people. Millions of pounds of clothing put on trains for the German people. Eyeglasses, teeth, shoes, everything. And when they loaded these trains, these two men hid themselves in the clothing, and on the way they jumped off. So they came running, city to city. And they came to the rabbi and told him that there is such a thing, it's called Treblinka, and they're killing all the Jews. And Treblinka, they said, was not far away at all, near the city of Krakow.

The rabbi said they are crazy. He could not believe them, he said, because that is impossible for human beings to behave in such a way.

Soon everybody was talking about it. Who did believe such a thing? Myself, I didn't think "yes" and I didn't think "no." People were saying they got letters from concentration camps that the Jews are doing heavy labour there, not given much to eat, but they are working, not killed. But later on started to come more stories, many more. We got used to the idea there is such a thing as killing camps, but we didn't want to believe it.

You understand, nobody knew how long the war is going to take. So everybody was thinking maybe another month, maybe another week, maybe another day. There were no ways and means to know the truth. There was even a Jewish paper, from Krakow, but under the supervision of the Germans. And that mislead the people.

On one occasion, one of the greatest Jewish theatre directors came to Pinczow, handing out bread to help the poor people. So nobody really knew for sure what's going to be — everybody thought, maybe it's going to go by, maybe only the younger people will be taken to work. They're taking away so many people — they're not going to kill just like that. Probably they're taking away to work.

Some people were optimistic and some pessimistic. But everybody did more or less know that *something* is going to happen. I don't know what I was thinking. I didn't believe that such a thing could happen — to take so many people and kill them. We didn't know about the ovens or something like that. But Treblinka was sitting in our head, because those two Jews talked about it, and we talked — maybe they're crazy, maybe it's propaganda, maybe they want something — but we didn't know what is what, because we were cut off from the world.

༒ FRANIA ༒

In the beginnning of April 1941, I was going out with Israel for these rendezvous, and it was very dangerous. The Germans, when they caught you, it was terrible. We had to go on sidestreets, we weren't allowed to go on the main streets. I wanted to get married, you know, very much. But I couldn't even talk to my parents — especially in the war, they didn't even want to hear about it. So I was very depressed — with the war going on, and this and that. There were different rumours: they took out already from a city all the Jews and we didn't even know where they took everybody. If to work, why don't they write? Why don't we hear anything? So different rumours were going around, and I was very depressed. And I suppose with this depression, and afraid of those Nazis — and my nerves were very very bad — I didn't have a nervous break-down but I remember one night I woke up and I started to scream: "I'm afraid, I'm afraid!" I was sleeping in the same room with Yossele, and I ran into his bed. So this was a sign that I am not well — after all, he was eighteen years old and I ran in into his bed. And he hugged me around, and I said, "I'm so afraid, I'm so afraid!" And I really wasn't feeling well. My parents, when they saw this, you know they saw that something happened, that I could really get a nervous breakdown or something. I remember the next day I was all day in bed. And my parents sent for Israel. It was the first time he was in my house. He came with his aunt Hadas. I remember it, they sat with me by the bed. So when he came naturally I felt much better. I was sick maybe just a few days and it went away.

Then it started again my rendezvous with Israel. I remember it was raining, it was a miserable day. It was around two o'clock, I made up to meet Israel somewhere.

My father came over to me and he said "So, daughter mine, what's going to be? You're going out with him again? It's raining outside. What's going to be?"

I said, "I'm asking you, Father. What's going to be? I want to get married."

He said, "Now? In the war you want to get married?"

"Yes. Now in the war I want to get married. I'm going around already with him five years and I want to get married. I don't care even if I'm going to be married one night. I want to be together one night. I want to get married."

You know if it would have been just up to my father, he would have helped a long time before, but my mother was very stubborn. She used to get so mad, her neck and chest got so red, it was terrible.

Well, my father said "Okay, okay — let's see. I'm coming with you and I'm going to talk to Israel."

So he went with me. When Israel saw from far away that I'm walking with my father, he got nervous. And I always told Israel, "We will go so long till my parents will tell me it's enough — I'm not going to do anything to hurt them, that's all." He very much understood this. Anyway my father went to him, and told me to go home, he wants to talk with Israel. Okay, I went home — and my mother knew, because she heard, but she didn't say a thing. I suppose she and my father talked about it already. So my father talked to Israel, and he started to like him.

When my father came home he said, "I talked to him, everything is fine, but how are you going to live? We hardly have to eat, what you're going to do?"

I said, "Look, Father, I'm not going to marry right away. I'm going to open myself a little store first, and if I'll see that I make something, we'll get married. But I want Israel should be able to come into our house, so I shouldn't be so miserable — at least this I deserve. Because I could have run away, and I wouldn't do that, so at least give me something too, I deserve."

You know, right away, as they say, he was laying down stones in front of me: "What do you mean you're going to open a store — where?"

I said, "Don't worry, I'll find something. That's my business."

"With what money — you haven't got a cent, and I can't give you — we hardly have enough for ourselves."

I told him I would go to my uncle, my mother's brother who lived twenty-seven kilometres away in a town called Dzialoszyce. He was very comfortable, he had money, he was dealing with grain, and he did very well. And he always had a soft spot for me.

I said, "I'm going to go to Uncle Itchele. He will give me money, so I'll buy a little bit of what I need: some pieces of soap, kerosene, a little bit of thread — things the farmers need, just necessities — a little coffee, sugar. I'll buy from a wholesale place and that's how I'll make a little money." A grocery store. But not a grocery store like here in Canada where everything is ready and in a package.

My father said, "How can you get a permit from the Germans?"

"Don't worry," I said, "I'll do everything."

The German headquarters for the area was in Busko Zdroj, sixteen kilometres from us — it was like a resort town. I knew a family there that used to live in Pinczow — the nicest people. He was a goldsmith and the Germans were going to him all the time for rings and jewellery. So I said I'll go to there — he always liked me — and with his contacts, that goldsmith is going to be able to get for me a permit. Otherwise you couldn't get it, you had to have a little side way to do it.

The first thing I had to see if I can find a store somewhere. There was a butcher shop, a widow owned it. It was closed up. The whole store was so big, like twice this kitchen — not even twice. And the walls, like in a butcher shop, were completely red. The widow told Israel and me she's going to rent us that store. She was a very good woman — she knew that we wanted to get married. Well, everybody in Pinczow knew that Schloime Baruch's daughter is running around with a young man, an actor. You know what this means? I can't even explain to you how bad this was, for a girl from a religious family. So fanatical but that was the way, that was the custom.

First I had to go to Dzialoszyce to my uncle Itchele. But you needed a permit to be allowed to go to another place. I wrote to that goldsmith in Busko, and he took out a special permit for me to be able to go out from Pinczow. I got on a wagon with a horse, and in Dzialoszyce my uncle didn't say a second word, he took out five hundred zlotys and gave me right away. I didn't get much for the money: I had to pay the widow rent right away for a month; we had to fix up the store a little bit — I had to paint over that red; and we went to that wholesale place to buy two kilograms of sugar, five pounds of salt, flour, some shoelaces, kerosene, salt, soap, some cotton, some thread, needles — just what the farmers might need right away. I remember in the beginning we couldn't buy much, so when we made that store, I put on the shelves empty boxes, it should look like we have some merchandise. But I don't have to tell you how friendly I am, and how friendly Israel is. When a farmer came into my store, he never walked out fast — we told him stories, and when we didn't have the thing, Israel ran fast to the wholesale place and bought it, while I kept the customer there with stories. And they wouldn't leave, they just loved us. After three months, that store was growing so fast, I didn't have where to put my merchandise any more, and the farmers, they were just crazy about us.

❦ ISRAEL ❦

One time came into the store two Wehrmacht soldiers. At seven o'clock you had to be at home because of the curfew. And they were sitting and talking because they were lonesome, they couldn't talk to the Poles — it's such a different language. But Yiddish is like German so to the Jews they could at least talk. They were quiet soldiers. They talked about their family in Germany. We asked them what they're doing with the Jews. They said, "We don't know anything." In the meantime, I saw it was after seven. I couldn't throw them out. I said we are scared to go home after curfew, they should take us home. First they said, "Oh no, we're not going to take you home." I start to talk to them, to their understanding, and they said, "You know what? We will go behind you, and you'll go forward, we will see." It just happened nobody caught us, that's all.

The most troubles we got was from the Poles, from our neighbours that our whole lives we lived side by side. They used to come in the store and to grab things and run away. "You're going to die just the same, what do you need it for?" And if we went out for a few minutes after the curfew — let's say somebody was a little bit late — the Poles brought the Germans, and said, "He went ten minutes after the curfew." The Germans didn't bother so much but the Poles were watching us like hawks.

It was hell. So if you are in hell, you cannot think normally. You think of two things: how the day was going to go by, and what to eat. The worst thing is, a human being when he's hungry. Cannot think.

I couldn't escape because I was with Frania. I could escape

by myself — my friends in Lodz asked me to go to Russia — but I didn't want to go without her. People thought that in Russia they will save themselves. But it was very hard to separate families. You could not do it just like that. An accident could happen and that's it, you're dead, and so is your family. People think an accident is happening to somebody else not them. The head was so blocked, you couldn't really think straight. You are thinking minute to minute, not what's going to be a day after. You only hoped the night would come. All day you were thinking about the night. Because only in the night was it a little bit easier to breathe. Every day you were expecting, every hour, something terrible will come, because every day the Germans issued new orders. And every day was something worse. Maybe today the war will be over, maybe tomorrow. A month, two months — because England is going in. America will go in. And especially we thought that Russia is strong. We never thought the war is going to take six years.

We were only wondering if, in the morning when we got up, will there be some new orders? Where am I going to be taken to work? What's going to happen? Everyday we went to work we didn't know if we'll come home at night. So what could you think? Every day we went to the store. We were thanking God the day is over, let's go home.

∽ FRANIA ∾

There was a woman, Zofia Banya was her name, she was a farmer's wife. You know, the farmers brought into the town eggs, butter, and then when they sold it, they bought kerosene, a piece of soap, shoelaces, things they need. They didn't eat what they grew — they ate just rye bread — and everything they had, they took to town to sell. Very poor farmers. A farmer there didn't have even a floor, it was just mud. Zofia Banya came once to the store, I remember, and she was short fifty groschen, which was less than a quarter. She was short but she needed the goods, so Israel said, "I'll lend you the money." There wasn't such a thing in Poland that you lend, credit. Nobody did it. And during wartime, forget about it. You could be not alive next week. And here she comes in, and Israel said to her, "You'll come next week, you'll bring me some butter, or some eggs, I'll take it off then. You need the things, so you're not going to go home without it. How you're going to manage during the week?" She couldn't forget that, that he trusted her. She could never forget it. In fact, if not for her, we wouldn't be alive today. So it's a two-way street.

After three months in the store, my father saw that I am doing so well, so we planned a wedding. You know, if you're in the religious way, before you get married, the girl has to go for a *mikveh* — a ritual bath — otherwise the rabbi doesn't give permission to get married. Well there, it's not like here, it was so filthy. And there was an old woman sitting there and to me, a young girl, she looked like a witch. You first of all have to cut your nails, a religious way, and the toenails too. So I did it myself before — I didn't want anyone else should ruin my nails for me. At that time, my hair I wore with one curl on top, it was stylish, and it suited me so nice. I had a long bobby pin and if you put it in, that curl was standing. So if I'm going to the *mikveh* there, I'll have to dip three times and to say the blessing — I'm going to lose that curl. First of all the old lady checked my nails, and cut two of them herself — and it was bleeding, that's the first thing — they didn't please her. That was first. And secondly, when I went into the water, you're not allowed to have a thing, all naked, like the way God made you, so you're not allowed to have a bobby pin in your hair. I took it out, and I was holding it tight in my hand, she shouldn't see. I figured the minute when I'll go out of the water, I'll stick it in right away, so I won't lose that curl. It was so filthy, that water — oh! All those old Chassidim used to go in there, and they splashed around there good. Anyway, I had to dip three times. Well, I dipped already three times, and when I went out, I was so alert, that I remembered my bobby pin and I stuck it in fast, and — she noticed. And when she noticed, she said, "It's not kosher." I had to go all over again. It was bad enough once to go, in that water. I had to do it twice. The witch, she noticed it, that's all.

A week before the wedding, Israel's grandfather — his mother's father, Michael Zawadzki, who was the rabbi in Busko Zdroj — sent a courier, that Israel should come to Busko to see him. He should take off his armband and come — imagine he asked him to risk his life. Listen, if the rabbi asked him to go…

Israel took off the armband, took a bicycle, went to his grandfather, and my heart was beating.

He went there, and the rabbi gave him the wedding ring — that I still have. He said, "This belonged to your mother and I want you to marry your wife with this ring. Remember, that whatever is going to happen, she should not lose this ring, and she should always take care, and watch nobody should take it away, and God will help, and you'll both be together alive." Those words.

Israel brought the ring back but it was big, and we had to go to a local goldsmith. His name was Kugiel — he was a little bit of a crazy little man. We asked Kugiel to make it smaller, he took the measurements, and said to leave it. So I said, "I can't leave it." He started to yell, "What do you mean, you're not trusting me? You can just leave altogether!" I said, "Look Kugiel, I want to tell you why, I want to tell you the story." When we told him the story, he was still mad. I said, "That's what the rabbi said, and I'm not going to leave it, you have to do it right away." Finally he quietened down a little bit, but he was still mad. Anyway, he made the ring smaller. I really watched out for that ring, whatever happened, and I still have it right here on my finger.

We got married in my house. I'll never forget that day: I woke up seven o'clock and it was raining, a storm. September usually is beautiful but there was such a storm, it was so dark, like night — and eight o'clock the same thing, and nine o'clock the same — it never stopped. And here I had a nice little dress, and a little veil, you know, to go down to the wedding. My grandmother comes to me, and she says "Don't worry yourself, at one o'clock, when you'll go under the wedding canopy, the sun will shine for you." That's what she said, and that's what happened. I had a pink dress, a beauty. Imagine, that dress was so lovely that later when I was pregnant and couldn't wear it, my sister Malkale took it and wore it in Warsaw — so beautiful was this dress. You know, I'm a good dresser, but I went special to another town, Kielce, to have that dress made. It was dusty pink, made from a light wool. I could picture it now.

Well, the sun came out and it was a gorgeous day. And that day a postcard came from Israel's father, wishing luck. And that was very unusual because at that time, the mail wasn't wonderful, believe me. And in Lodz was already a ghetto, that's why it was such a miracle that this postcard came.

So we got married, and we lived with my parents. They gave us one room, and we lived there. In the morning, we went to the store. Right after we got married, I said to Israel, "You know what — I think I'm going to start baking little rolls, cookies. Because the farmers come Sundays to town for church or to visit sick people, friends, or family. So we're going to be making a fortune on these cookies and the rolls I bake." I made those rolls and everything, and we were selling, like hotcakes.

I was baking the cookies and rolls for our store at the bakery next door, they let me do it. Well, in '42 it was a freezing winter, and I suppose I got very warm there at the bakery. When I went out, I caught a cold or something, and I took sick. And really sick; I had typhus. There was a small epidemic of it. Six people — I remember them all — were taken to the hospital. The minute they took them to the hospital, they died. We had a family doctor, a little old man, such a nice man, he said he's not going to take me to the hospital. But you're not allowed to be at home when you have typhus. He said, "I'm going to say it's something else: scarlet fever. We're not going to take her to the hospital, because there she has no chance." I was very thin too. I probably didn't weigh more than ninety pounds. My father was the only one allowed in the room with me. Israel wanted to see me, he had to go to the window to look in — my father didn't allow anybody inside the room. Three months after I got married, I was that sick. I remember, there was a table there, the whole table was full of medicine. Then I started to lose my hair. The doctor begged me I should shave off my head, and I didn't want to. I made a mistake, because I wouldn't have such thin hair now. But I would lose everything if not for my brother Chamel in Lublin: he was sending the best medicine to rub into your scalp. I was so sick three months, that after that I had to be carried on the chair on pillows.

At that time the trouble started with my brother Yossele. We didn't have any money, and Yossele — he was then 17 — wanted to smuggle things from one town to the other. You could smuggle things like peas, or potatoes, things like that. Jews weren't allowed to go from city to city: the minute they caught you outside Pinczow, they could shoot you right away. Anyway, Yossele went with his friend Zavel on bicycles to smuggle. So I remember my father used to say, "Yossele, this friend is not for you." My father told him that Zavel was maybe nice, but his father was a horse dealer — considered lower class in Poland. My father warned that Zavel has got the character from his parents, he is brought up in that house, but Yossele wanted to make some money. He had a bicycle and they smuggled already twice. Still my father warned him: "I don't like you should go with Zavel, this friend is not for you."

Meanwhile my brother Yossele had to take off his armband to go smuggling, and he didn't look Jewish at all — he looked exactly blond like Shaindele — he looked like a Gentile. His friend Zavel, you could see he's Jewish from his features.

Yossele could have smuggled by himself. He was so tall and so beautiful, so handsome, blond.

Anyway, they caught Zavel. Why did he need they should catch Yossele too? You're going to be happy if they're going to shoot him too? Zavel told the German right away: "This is my friend, he is Jewish too."

My father warned Yossele about that boy.

They put them both in jail, and they wanted to shoot them both, right away. But Shaindele was going everywhere with money she got from Chamel from Lublin. What she did, it's unbelievable. First of all you had to go to the German authorities for paper that allowed you to travel from one town to the other — you couldn't just go out of town, as a Jewish girl. So she got this. How, I don't know. Because you had to have connections to get this paper. So she could travel. There was a main office in Radom — from there they gave orders to the small towns. Even so far as Radom went Shaindele. She got to the secretary of…I don't remember who exactly, but some important man, a German, and she paid him a fortune. How she got to him — she was very intelligent, she had a way how to do it, you know. Personality. That man promised her that when the execution papers of Yossele and Zavel came up, he would put them on the bottom. Shaindele made such contacts with the jail people in Pinczow, that Yossele could send out letters, and we could send in some food to him. I'll never forget when he wrote once in a letter that each time he heard the key going around, he thought that's it: they're taking him out already to be shot. Imagine. Later they took him to Kielce, forty kilometres away from Pinczow. A few months later, they took out all the Jews from Kielce for the deportation to the camps, so naturally they took out everybody from the jail too. Anyone that had a death sentence was handcuffed, and the feet too. A lot of people were jumping the train — some are alive today. Some got shot, it's true, but who could run away fast sometimes lived. Yossele, the poor thing, he couldn't jump. How could he jump, if he was tied here and tied there? He couldn't. So he was taken away on the train to Majdanek, and killed. Never mind killed — at Majdanek they burned.

By April '42 I was already pregnant. The store was still going. The Germans came to our store, not once, to look. You weren't allowed to sell cigarettes. Or flints for lighters. If they would find this, right away they would close the store. They could shoot me too. So Israel made a little wooden chair with a seat that could open like a lid, and there inside was everything. There was one SS, when I saw him coming into the store, I was just shaking. He was sitting in that chair, the German. You had to risk, what could you do, you couldn't help it, you made money on that.

࿔ ISRAEL ࿔

We were in the store around six o'clock in the evening, we wanted to close it. The murderer of the city comes in. That murderer killed every day two, three people. In the street, walking in the street, took out his gun and shot, just for fun and laughed. Jews mostly. Whoever got an armband. We wanted to close the store and he came in with another soldier, an SS man. When I saw him, I got white, I couldn't stand still, and I asked him very politely, "What can I do for you?" So he said, "You will give me two batteries for my flashlight." He gave me the flashlight, I turned around, I just could not put the batteries into the flashlight, so much my hands were shivering. I just could not put it in straight. Just couldn't do it. And if you showed that in a movie, people would say it's exaggerated. The fear said: now is the end — because we did know him, what kind of man this was. He yelled at me, "You dirty Jew, why can't you do it?" He took it from my hands and did it himself and he started to curse. Then he looked around to see what else he could take, and walked out. It took probably ten minutes, but those ten minutes were ten years. Impossible to describe.

ᥱᡠ᠊ FRANIA ᠊ᡠᥱ

Later they put in a commissar, like an overseer into our store — imagine, to that little store. They saw that we're selling so much, so they put in a commissar, because there was always a line-up outside. How much people liked us. I didn't have where to put my money any more — so much money we made that later my brother didn't even send money, I already had money for my father too. Well, the commissar had control: we made so much and he took so much. Then we had to take out already these hidden things from the chair.

Anyway, by that time it was nearly at the end. People started to say that soon they're going to take the Jews out of Pinczow. They took from other cities, we heard. You know Dzialoszyce, where my uncle was that gave the money to open the store, we heard they took out all the Jews already from there. They left only the Jewish committee, the *Judenrat*. They asked my father to be on that committee in Pinczow, and he didn't want to — he was lucky that they didn't force him. If you were on the *Judenrat* you had to do all the filthy work to your own brother and sister. You know what happened in Warsaw: there was on the committee there a doctor and a wife, and they asked him, let's say, in a week's time, to give ten thousand children, such and such an age. So how could he give ten thousand children? They found him and the wife both dead in the morning — they committed suicide — he couldn't do it with his own hands, to give them ten thousand children.

We heard about Dzialoszyce, and about other cities too. You see, we knew already that they're not taking the Jews to work, because people were saying you never heard about them any more. You know, bad news travels fast. A lot of people took off the armbands, went from town to town, and that's the way the news spread around. We knew they take the younger people to work, and the older people they take right away in concentration camp. We didn't know exactly, but we knew plenty. We knew that the people vanish, that's all. Vanish. And people were saying: it's getting hot, it's getting hot. That was already by May '42. And the life was going on quietly — it was a small town. In big cities, it was worse. In Pinczow we didn't have so many Germans.

In Lublin was already the deportation. The grandfather was already gone, they took him to concentration camp. How could my brother Chamel help him? — it happened so suddenly. During the night, they circle around the ghetto, and they take out the Jews — the grandfather and everybody.

So after this, whoever was left — the police, *Judenrat*, or Jews who had a special job — the Germans kept these people in the Lublin ghetto. These Jews had a passport marked with a "J" and they didn't have to be deported to camps. Yet. Naturally my brother — I told you how smart he was — he was working for the Germans, so he had the "J." Letters weren't going any more, so Chamel called by the telephone and said he's going to make first a "J" passport for mother. He's going to send a courier, a Gentile man — he had lots of friends there — and he's going to bring Mother to that little ghetto in Lublin. We never thought that these Jews in Lublin will be safe forever there, but listen, we were hoping that maybe tomorrow the war will be finished. In the meantime we just wanted to stretch time to be alive, you understand?

Well, a man came, and he took Mother by train to Chamel. She travelled as a Gentile, without the armband. That was already, I think, in August — you know, time in the meantime flies. And for the rest of us — I'm telling you, his head worked good — for us Chamel made "J" passports that we were already Lublin Jews, in case something happens in Pinczow.

You know, the Germans were like this: if he comes here to Ottawa to arrest Saul Rubinek, but you have a passport you are from Toronto — so he doesn't arrest you, because he has to arrest you right in Toronto. They were just going straight like a horse: you asked them to kill, they kill, just like that. Not to kill, also fine.

So Chamel made us those passports, with the "J," for me, and for Israel, and my father, and for Malkale, and for Shaindele.

We were waiting. We knew already it's getting hot. We heard about deportations in one city, then another, and another. It's getting hot.

I told you when we rebuilt the house, we left the burned store in front, and where windows used to be in the front of the store, was filled in with stones. Between the stones you could peek out and see the square, the whole square. When people started to say it's so hot, Israel started to dig in that part where the store was, and made a bunker for us to hide in. He dug up a hole, and he covered it. There were stairs there from the burned-out store to the basement — the last step was where he made a big bunker.

It was September, the Jewish New Year — Rosh Hashanah — and I'll never forget it: I was already in charge in place of mother, so I had to cook. We were sitting and having gefilte fish, and all of a sudden we hear German voices, *"Raus! Raus! Raus! Raus!"* We fast ran to the bunker, me and Israel, my father, Malkale, and Shaindele. Also there was a couple, their name was Gurski, who knew about the bunker, because the husband, Yitzchak Gurski, was president of Pinczow's *Judenrat*. We made an agreement with Gurski that if the time ever comes that we have to go and hide in the bunker, we'll hide his wife and daughter.

As a *Judenrat* president he would not be deported with everyone else. The Nazis used the *Judenrat* to do their dirty work, so the agreement was when the coast was clear, Gurski would come tell us to come out of the bunker. We had to take them in — his wife and their beautiful little daughter, four years old.

Seven of us sitting there in that hole. I was already six months pregnant.

The way Israel made that bunker, it was a masterpiece: he covered it with pieces of wood, and on that put cement and clay — everything so covered up, you couldn't tell it was there. But it wasn't big, it wasn't meant for so many people. We could stand up in it, and we had there small little chairs. We didn't have any food — we just ran straight down there — we didn't know for how long. We thought that when night comes we'll run away through the woods to another town. Later Chamel would take us to Lublin. The first thing: we shouldn't go with that deportation.

Israel's grandmother, and his two aunts, they were in their own house — we couldn't tell everybody about our bunker. His aunt Hadas got married just before. She was, oh, such an intelligent woman, and a heart of gold, you never seen such a person like she was. But we could not tell her, because she was with her husband, and then there was his aunt Surele — she was so sick with her heart that she had probably four heart attacks before the war — and her three children, and a husband, and then the grandmother. So where would we put them? That bunker was even not big enough for us. Imagine what was going on. Till this day Israel can't forgive himself for his aunt Hadas. But how could you help it? Oh! it was terrible.

✺ ISRAEL ✺

My aunt Hadas I'm never going to forget as long as I'm going to live. She was absolute a human being — a *mensch*. I never met

– and I'm not so young – a human being like her: so understanding and so much the kind who would give a hand and help. A saint. All right, I was only a teenager then, a boy, and she was in her thirties. And today I'm sixty-eight and still I met nobody like her. But about my aunt Hadas let me be very cool: I believe very strongly that sometimes I understand things and it's very hard for me to bring it out with my mouth. And sometimes I accuse myself about being too sure of what I think and understand. Anyway I have considered very deeply if it's possible to think the same way today as I used to think in that time. I'm making a survey: what would I think if I would be eighteen years old now? I wouldn't change my mind. Because it was not an erotic love – if it would be erotic love it can make blind, I want you to know that – and human love is different: you can fall in love with an eighty-year-old, as a human being. I have not changed my mind about my aunt Hadas. I saw how she behaved to people, believe me.

⟬ FRANIA ⟭

We were seven people in that bunker, sitting there. It was quiet. Later they came, the Germans. The Poles told them to look for the Greenfeld family. Who didn't know us in Pinczow? We heard them screaming outside on the square: "Where are the Greenfelds? Where are the Greenfelds?" The Germans were yelling, and then they ran down the stairs – right on top of us they were standing, I'll never forget that. Oh! you were afraid to breathe. Just plain breathe. The little girl there, she didn't make a sound. You know, crisis makes you understand so much, it's unbelievable. A little child of four understood already how to behave. So we heard everything, hiding under the Germans' feet. "Where are they?!" in German they were yelling and screaming. But they couldn't find us.

Anyway, when we heard already it's quiet, it's quiet, Israel said to my father, "I'll go up, I'm going to look through the stones and see what's happening in the square – to see if they're taking out Jews, or what."

It must have been five, six o'clock – we were down there five hours already, since lunchtime – now it was quiet. So I was afraid he should go out, God forbid if there somebody will see him.

He said, "Who could see me? If it's quiet now, nobody will see me. The store is burned, and through the stones maybe I'll see something."

Imagine, he went out. Israel went out, and it took probably fifteen minutes – it was like fifteen years – till I saw him back.

He came back, and did he cry, did he cry. He told us the whole square was full of Jews, and in the first row he saw his grandfather, the rabbi, from Busko Zdroj. From Busko Zdroj was sixteen kilometres. The Germans were chasing them by foot to Pinczow, all the Jews from Busko. Imagine. And his grandfather was in the first row. Oh, he was a handsome man, he was such a handsome man, the rabbi. Israel saw him in the first row standing, half his beard torn from him. Can you imagine how he felt? All the Jews he saw, Israel cried, were standing just like they're going to a slaughterhouse. Oh, he cried for hours. And we were sitting there, and we knew what's going on, and we knew already that they took his aunt, and his grandmother, and everybody. And we sit there, for what? What do I have to look forward to?

We were hoping that the Polish police captain, Kopecz, would come with Gurski to tell us when it's okay to come out. You see, Gurski and I promised him money to do it. He'll tell us when it's quiet, after they're going to take out all the Jews – they took them all out probably with trucks – who knows what, we didn't see, and didn't hear, we were in that hole, sitting there. It must have been two o'clock in the morning, Kopecz came. You know what? He didn't come with Gurski. I think, at the last minute, they took Gurski with the deportation. Kopecz came with Israel's best friend Shmulek Finer, who was Captain of the Jewish Police in Pinczow. He knew where we were hiding. So Kopecz came with Shmulek there at night, and we hear all of a sudden in Polish, Kopecz's voice:

"Children get out. Get out — it's quiet now."

We opened that little cover, and all went out.

"Where's my husband?" said Gurski's wife.

Shumlek Finer said "I don't know."

Kopecz said, "They took out all the Jews. Nobody's left."

☜ ISRAEL ☞

I went quietly out of the bunker, up the stairs, and I peeked between the stones to look out on the square. Hundreds of Jews. Everybody was standing like mummies. Just stunned. Like a stone is quiet. The only thing that's still ringing in my ears, and as long as I'm going to live it will ring in my ears, how the Poles were laughing.

"It's an end of the Jews. The Jews are going to be fried in the ovens."

I'll never forget that. I don't know who is interested in it, but I'll never forget that laughter, the devilish laughter from all the best friends, neighbours, that lived with us for hundreds of years.

"Better tell me where you hide your gold, because you're going to die just the same."

I saw on that square all the Jews gathered together from Pinczow and Busko and Wislica, and the Poles were walking around there between the Germans, and yelling, and laughing. It happened all the time. When they came into a store, they asked to give them for nothing because, "Just the same you're going to leave it, why you're not giving to me?" And we said, "Hitler starts with the Jews, but will end with you — have you got your Poland?"

❦ FRANIA ❦

Now the best thing, we thought, was to run to Dzialoszyce. They had there already the deportation but they left a few Jews from the *Judenrat* and the Jewish police, and their families. Imagine, for me, pregnant, to go through woods to Dzialoszcye — thirty kilometres. But what could I do? I'm not going to die here.

So we started to run through sidestreets, nobody should see us. Me, Israel, my father, Shaindele, and Malkale. Gurski's wife and her little girl wanted to go somewhere else, so we separated. In the middle of the night, we started to cut through the woods — Israel knew exactly how to go.

Suddenly, two Germans — I don't know from where they came — "Halt!" Can you imagine? "Where do you think you're going? Who are you?" They wanted to kill us right away, after all the other Jews were already taken away, right away they shot you. We took out our "J" passports, and showed them that we are from Lublin, not Pinczow, it just happens that we were here. One was standing with his rifle ready to shoot us, that minute. But the other one — it's my impression he was sent from God — was an angel. I could recognize him now, a beautiful face he had, and a good face, I'm telling you, a Messiah. He said, "We have no right to shoot Lublin Jews." So the other one, the bad one, said, "What else do you want to do with them?" They decided to take us back to the Pinczow jail. One was an angel and the other one was just a devil. He saw that I am pregnant, but when we started to walk back to Pinczow, he took his rifle and hit me over my feet — the bad one, not the good one. I was already in my seventh month, and I fell over, and he hit me again. He made me all full of marks, blue marks. Only me, he hit. Just me. So the other one yelled at him, he shouldn't do it, he tried to stop him.

✑ *ISRAEL* ✑

Before the first war, there was a judge living in Pinczow, he was a Russian. When the Russians went out of Poland — Poland reclaimed it in 1918 or so — that judge still was sitting in Pinczow and he became a Polish citizen. Once upon a time, he was sitting on the bench, and he got mad about something, and he said, "You are all a bunch of Polish swine." Naturally, the Poles took him off the bench. He became practically a beggar. But later he opened a notary office, and people paid him for writing official letters. He was highly intelligent. But he became an alcoholic. He did everything you wanted — for a few zlotys. One time, he came into our store, and I asked him if it would be possible he should make me a false passport — from a dead person, or somebody — so that maybe someday, I will be able to run away from the Germans as a Pole. I paid him and he made me an official passport with my photograph and he gave me the name Josef Lewitski. When we were caught in the woods running out of Pinczow, I showed them this Polish passport. I didn't have the "J" passport like the others.

At the Pinczow police station one of the Poles there said, "That is a Jew. He is the son-in-law of the Greenfelds." I remember him, that bastard. His name was Yustonarski. He also told the Germans we are all from Pinczow. But it was our luck there were Ukrainians there, and Poles and Germans, and one couldn't understand what the other one was saying.

✑ *FRANIA* ✑

Anyway, they took us to the Pinczow jail. That was quite a walk.

And who was in jail? Other Jews too made different hiding places, and after they took out all the Jews, if they still found somebody, some of them they shot right away, and they took some to the jail. Why to jail? If there's going to be, let's say, a deportation in another town, they'll take us there.

We were sitting there, I think a day or two. We didn't know what's going to happen with us. And one morning, they came in: *"Raus!"*

They put us all on a wagon. They caught quite a few Jews after the deportation. There were probably ten wagons with horses. Polish farmers were the drivers. Where do you think the Germans get the wagons? They go to the farmers and force them to give it for nothing. One of the farmers told us the Germans are taking us to the jail in Stopnic. Israel's uncle — his father's brother-in-law Moishe Ehrlichman — lived in Stopnic and he had a store there. We thought that if we could get out of the Stopnic jail, we'll have where to go.

In Poland, the roads were very bad, and everywhere deep ditches. We were already out of Pinczow, it was in the morning, suddenly my father said to Shaindele — I'll never forget it — "Shaindele, jump."

We had wagons behind us, but they were all Jewish people, and all from our city, they wouldn't give us away. And the farmers, you think they liked the Germans?

My father said to her, "The German doesn't look now, you just jump, and go right into the ditch, save your life."

She said, "I don't care, I don't care for my life. If you are all gone, I'm not going to have anybody. I won't do it. Don't talk like this."

He said, again, "I'm telling you jump. Why should we all go from this world? At least one will be alive."

She said no.

And why did he ask her? Because she looked like a Gentile, she never looked Jewish, never. But she said no. So the minute we went where the road was narrow, and there was a big ditch there, very deep — and she didn't realize that my father will do a thing like this — when the German wasn't looking, my father gave Shaindele a push and threw her down off the wagon. That's guts. You think about it. She couldn't even yell out, the minute the German would see, right away he would shoot her. So she couldn't help it, she had to hide in the ditch. The other wagons saw this too, but nobody said a word, and she was hidden there in that ditch. Later we heard that when everything went by, she just walked away in the fields to another town. She had money — we all had money with us. My father, right away when something happened, gave everybody money — a few hundred zlotys. Because if he gets separated from us, we should at least have something to live on. So Shaindele bought a train ticket, and went to Lublin. She knew Chamel's address but she didn't want to go into the ghetto, she wanted to go to Warsaw. She knew where Chamel is working, and she waited for him there. Imagine when he saw her there in Lublin. Right away he made for her papers saying she is a Pole, and right away she was prepared to go to Warsaw.

When we came to Stopnic, they again put us in jail. There wasn't yet the deportation in Stopnic, so they locked us up to wait for the deportation. And this jail I'll never forget in my life. The jail in Pinczow was at least very big. You wanted to go to the bathroom, they let you go. But here we were probably two hundred — there were some already from before too — in two little rooms, but it was like a basement. I didn't have with what to breathe there, I thought I'm going to faint. There was a window there, but it was high and on a slant. So Israel and my father were holding me up to the window so I shouldn't slide down, and I was getting some air there through the steel bars.

We were sitting there, I think, two days, and it was just impossible. Why? Because there wasn't a bathroom, so everybody was making on the floor. Can you imagine sitting there in that shit — excuse my expression. It was impossible, it was unbearable.

Soon they're going to take us to concentration camps but we

knew one thing: if you're young, if you're still healthy, they take you first to work, they don't burn you right away. Everybody wanted to work, because meanwhile you have a hope that the war will finish and you'll still be alive. So everybody wanted to look young. My father had a beard — he was a very handsome man, my father — but a beard makes everybody look older. Anyway, in that dirt there, in that filth there was a bottle, and Israel took the bottle and broke it — I'll never forget this moment in my life — with that piece of glass he shaved my father. He was shaving him, and we were all crying, the tears were just coming down. We wanted him to look younger, they should not murder him right away, they should take him to work. In the middle of that filth, he shaved all his beard off. You know, he looked probably twenty years younger, and he was so handsome, I'm telling you.

There was a Polish officer at the jail, he was a higher rank than a policeman — and I say the same thing, it was an angel sent from God — you know, if you have faith, you believe in it. He came the first night and then the second night he came too. He saw me pregnant, my father and my husband holding me up to that window, that I cannot breathe, and so much filth there on that floor. When he came, always he said these words: "How are you children?" Just like that — like a father coming to see how his children are. Israel gave him the idea that if we don't get out, we are all of us going to be sick with typhus and that will cause an epidemic. That's what they were afraid of, the Germans: if it's an epidemic, they're going to catch it too. Let us out, we'll wash, at least we'll be clean and when they deport the city, we'll go anyway. That's what the Polish officer told the Germans and I suppose the Germans saw that it's logical. In the morning they let us out.

We went right away to Israel's uncle, Moishe Ehrlichman. His house was together with the business — everywhere was like this in Poland, specially in the small towns. His store was already closed — the Germans took everything there, it was almost empty. And listen, who had patience to run a store anyway? When Israel's aunt saw me, she took me into the store, and she locked the door. She gave me a big, big pot, and hot water she warmed up on the stove, and I got undressed, and I washed up. And I felt like alive again. You know, when you're in the dirt, you don't think. And Israel washed up, and my father, and Malkale. Then Israel's aunt cooked potatoes with red borscht — I'll never forget the taste, how good this was.

We started to think already again. You're clean again, you are not hungry. You started to live again and to think: why should I wait for the deportation? Maybe there is still something I can do. We wanted to save a little bit our life, to stretch it.

We ran to a phone and called Chamel in Lublin. We were all day on that telephone. We told him everything that happened to us and he said the first thing for us to do was to go to Dzialoszyce — we should not go with the deportation right here, in Stopnic. In Dzialoszyce was still there my uncle Itchele — the uncle who gave me the five hundred zlotys to open the store — and there was still left the police, and a few Jews with their families. From there Chamel said he would be able make arrangements to take us to Lublin.

Israel
It was sixty kilometres from Stopnic to Dzialoszyce. We couldn't just go to any farmer for a horse and wagon because instead of taking you, he could take you right away to the Germans, and for each head he'll get two kilograms of sugar.

Frania
So we had to have a responsible man, we couldn't go with just anybody.

Israel
We called Dzialoszyce to her uncle Itchele, and he sent a farmer he trusted with a horse and wagon. He came at night, right to the door. It was an open wagon full of hay, and the two sides was like a ladder.

Frania

Israel and my father hid in the straw, and Malkale and me, we sat on top with the farmer. The Germans would see a farmer and two women, they wouldn't stop us but with the men also sitting there it would be too dangerous. And this farmer took us by sideroads, to be even safer. In the middle of the woods, all of a sudden a few Poles, hooligans, came running out: "Stop the wagon!" and they started to search what we have. Right away when I saw them running out of the woods, I knew that I have to save my wedding ring — I took it off and put it under my tongue. But they took my watch, and I had a little brooch, and from Malkale they took things too. And they didn't look in the hay. This was very lucky. Then they ran away.

Israel

Sure we were lucky. Because they knew that we are Jewish. They were yelling to the farmer: "You're a traitor. You're saving Jews." They looked in the faces and they recognized Jews.

Frania

They knew. Sure. If you go with a wagon with two girls and you don't even try to stop them…In those days everybody knew — you don't have to be smart for that. But they just wanted to steal, that's all.

Israel

We came to Dzialoszyce, straight to Itchele.

Frania

My uncle Itchele had a wife and two daughters and a son, Leibick, he was sixteen.

Israel

But when we came from Stopnic to Dzialoszyce, his wife and daughters were already gone. He didn't know if they are killed. He didn't know anything.

Frania

They were taken right away in the first deportation, only he and Leibick were left. But my grandparents were staying there — they were there already before the deportation in Pinczow. Why not? Itchele was their son — my mother's brother. We called Chamel right away. He told us Shaindele was already together with him in Lublin — that she was alive was a miracle — and he's sending her to Warsaw as a Pole. But first he wants to make arrangements to bring Malkale to Lublin so both sisters can go to Warsaw together. He said he wants to take us all to Lublin. Next my father. But me — I couldn't go. A pregnant woman could not be allowed in the ghetto there after they already had the first deportation. That's that. And that was the luck that they couldn't take me. Because if they took me to Lublin, I wouldn't be here either, and neither would you my son, because from Lublin ghetto they took everybody to Majdanek, and everybody died there, in the gas chambers.

Israel

Then Frania's father took me aside — he was crying — and he told me, "It is a time that you have to think sober. Normal. We know that probably nobody of us will stay alive. Run. You don't look specifically Jewish, so run away." So I told him, "I don't care very much for my life. If I had to save my life, I could have saved it before the war — my friends wanted me to go with them to Russia, they all went to Russia. And I didn't want to save myself. Later on if I'll stay alive I…no! I just cannot do that. What's going to happen to you? And with the rest? If I can help — I feel I can help — and if I can help I'll stay and I am not running away from my responsibilities." He tried very hard to persuade me, but I didn't want to talk any more about it. I didn't want he should have the power to persuade me, so I cut it off.

Frania

My father went to Israel and said to him, "Don't stick with
your wife. She is my daughter, but if you're going to hold
on to her, you're going to die together with her. You look
like a Gentile, you were travelling without the armband
so many times, and nobody would dare go and ask if you
are Jewish. Go to a farm, run away, take off the armband,
and save your life." So Israel said, "I don't care — if I
haven't got Frania, I don't care to live. I don't care, I don't
give a damn." That's what he said. So my father — who
can forget it? — came to me — and I was already eight
months pregnant — and he said, "My daughter, I talked to
Israel, he doesn't want to listen to me, but talk to him."

Israel

No. Your father didn't talk to you about it.

Frania

What do you mean? My father came to me and told me, "I
couldn't persuade your husband. You talk to him, you're
his wife and he loves you and he's going to listen to you."
You see how I remember? You know why Israel doesn't
remember? Because when my father talked to him, it
went in one ear and went out the other. Israel doesn't like
to talk about the unpleasant things. But it's part of life.
Life is just candies? Anyway, my father said to me, "The
minute they have the deportation, right away they separate
husband and wife. You're not going to be with him even
one minute. What good will it be if he is going to be dead
too? Persuade him, talk to him, he should run away, he
should save his life. Look, I saved Shaindele's life, I threw
her down from the wagon. You think I don't know how
you feel?" So I saw he is talking sense. He wouldn't be with
me a minute if we would go to the deportation. So I went
to Israel, and I talked to him, I said, "Father is right —
what's the point? You're going to die together with me —

not even together." So he said, "Would you do it, if you were me?" I said, "How could I do it, I cannot run." He said, "Just tell me, would you do it, if you could?" So I didn't answer. What could I answer? So he said, "That's all. I don't want to talk about it. It's not even fair that you're asking me such a question. And don't talk to me, because nothing will help."

⟿ FRANIA ⟾

Then after a few days a man came to bring Malkale to Lublin. I can picture him now: a handsome man with personality, a Pole, in his sixties. I remember when Malkale left Dzialoszyce, a friend of my uncle, a very smart man, said that Malkale is going to need luck: she has a Yiddish *cheyn*, that means she has a Jewish flavour. You know, Malkale, she's a good-looking girl, and at that time, when she was fifteen, can you imagine how she was beautiful. He said, "Oh! I'm afraid for that Yiddish *cheyn*."

Then right away after Malkale, Chamel sent for my father, and if my father wouldn't go, he would be alive today, because he would have been safe with us. So my father had to go, and leave me. But my father had a policy that it was such a war, that you had to see that whatever life you could save, to save. If you stayed together, you died together. And that's why he threw down Shaindele from the wagon too. If he wouldn't, who knows what would happen.

Again that Gentile man came and took my father to Lublin. Just before he left, my father asked my uncle to try to arrange for a farmer to hide us — and my grandparents were there too.

So I said, "Hide with a farmer who doesn't know me at all?" He is going to hide my uncle Itchele — the farmers know him for so many years, they were dealing with him in grain — but with me, he's going to hold me a day, take the money away, and later he is going to kill me too. Or he is going to throw me out, if he doesn't know me at all.

"Yes," my father said, "but it's possible that the war will finish tomorrow." You understand, we just had that hope: it's going to finish tomorrow. Like a dream.

A few days after my father left, a woman I knew from Pinczow — her name was Rivcze — came with her family to Dzialoszyce. She had two daughters: one was fourteen, and she had a little girl, a retarded child, very little she was — she was already probably eight, but she looked three, you understand. And her husband was very tall and thin, and a little bit cuckoo — one little screw was missing. But Rivcze was very smart, and she was a very good friend of ours — she used to be in our house more than her own. She came to Dzialoszyce to my uncle Itchele, she knew him from Pinczow yet.

When she saw me, she said, "Oh my God, what are you doing here?"

I said, "What do you mean what I'm doing? What does everybody do?"

She said, "You know what happened? From where we come now? We were at a farmer's place hidden. Ludwig Banya. And his wife Zofia was running all over the woods looking for you. She said she wants to save the life of the young couple, the Rubineks. Where are they?"

The Poles said that we weren't at the deportation, you understand? They didn't see the whole family Greenfeld.

Ludwig's farm was just outside Pinczow. When it was the time of the Pinczow deportation, Rivcze and her family, like a lot of other people, ran into the woods to hide. But later on, they had to eat. So they started to go to the farmers to sleep over or to get food. And that's how Rivcze ended up at Ludwig and Zofia's. But they were thrown out of there because Ludwig couldn't keep four people hidden — he could be shot too. Rivcze and her husband and the two daughters ran at night through the woods to Dzialoszyce.

When we heard that Zofia was looking for us, well — you had to be a diplomat at that time. You couldn't say, "Oh really, I'm going to run to that farm" — you couldn't say that, you had to think about yourself. You were so selfish, you know. If you said something, right away you had another three people wanted to go with you — so then the farmer wouldn't take in a whole army. I didn't say a thing. I just listened. And Israel too — we just listened.

Later I took my uncle to the side, I said, "Why should I go to one of your farmers who I don't even know. If she came, Rivcze, and she tells me that Zofia was running all over, she wants to save us — why shouldn't I go to somebody who is looking for me, somebody I know?"

And I remembered that Zofia was so thankful that Israel credited her that few cents that time, trusted her, you understand. But how would I get there? How do I know she still wants me?

So Uncle Itchele said, "You know what, I'm going to send somebody on a bicycle to her place, we will let her know that you are alive, and she should come here to Dzialoszyce, we will talk with her, and then we'll see." Fine. So he found a young fellow — see, he knew nice people, there were Poles that were nice people too, you know. Not many, but there were some, like any other nation. This young fellow never gave us away. He took a bicycle, and he rode half a day to Banya's farm, with a letter from us. He came back and said that he found Zofia in the stable, painting, and she almost fell off the ladder when she heard that we are alive. And she said she is coming tomorrow. And how is she coming? — by foot. And decided that Israel will wait at the post office.

Next day Israel was waiting there, and waiting and waiting — and he didn't see her. If she made her mind up she's going to come, and he was there all day, and she didn't come, so listen, she probably backed out, she changed her mind. She's afraid, or something, and that's it.

Meantime in Dzialoszyce it started already to get hot. That

means, people were saying: any day — tomorrow — it's going to be the deportation. They come five o'clock in the morning — "*Raus, raus, raus!*" and it's finished. Imagine, that already I prepared myself to go with the deportation. I felt I don't want to go to a strange farmer — what's the point? Israel didn't want to run away, he wanted me. So we already started to get ready. I remember I took a kerchief, and I put in some sugar, and some candies, I should have something prepared for the deportation when we go. And *qué sera*, what can I do? Nothing.

Israel
First of all, there was already a deportation a few weeks before. But some Jews ran away. Later on the Germans put out posters that all the Jews in hiding can come back and make a new life. So they came back. Because it was so chaotic, so unbelievable nobody knew what happened in other places — and what happened to the people, nobody did know. There were Jewish policemen, and the Germans told them there's going to be another deportation, and so people were preparing every day. They didn't know when. They prepared parcels — they didn't know where they were going — to work. So what did they prepare? Bread, water, and clothing. And everybody was waiting for the deportation. And us too. Once and for all, we didn't know for sure that we're going to die.

Frania
We thought they're taking us to work.

Israel
That's what I'm fighting now with people: everybody that says that we didn't fight back. If I believe I'm going to work, why should I die?

Frania
That's why we shaved my father — because we didn't know what they did to the older people, that they just go and burn, just like that.

Israel

First of all, you have to go by ABC: we didn't have any news, only the German paper — the Polish paper was under the supervision of the Germans — so we didn't know anything. But the older Jews said, "We remember the first war, the Germans took everybody to work. They didn't kill, it's just propaganda." Plain. But some people read Hitler's book *Mein Kampf* and they said, "The Jews are not going to live." Other people said, "The world would not allow it." So everybody wanted to believe that they're being taken to work. Because the Germans did like this: they took people to the concentration camp and forced them to write letters home. And letters came: "We are working and everything is all right." In fact, in Pinczow once, a letter came from a man, a water-carrier, who was blind, and couldn't read and couldn't write — from him a letter came. So people said that he must have asked somebody to write the letter for him. You see, we wanted to believe that way.

Discussions were going on that the Germans are not going to kill all the people. We knew that they were killing cripples, and the old. There were discussions about politics. We were counting on politics — it's impossible for one nation to go against the whole world. First of all, we were sure that we knew the Russians — that the Communists are against Germany and when they got into the war...

Frania

One, two, three, it's finished.

Israel

Two days, a week, two weeks. The thing to do is just to wait it out for a few weeks, till it's over.

Frania

So when Zofia didn't show up, we resigned ourselves

already to go with the deportation. And then it took another few days, and I said to Israel and to my uncle, "What do I have to lose, why should I go with the deportation? Who knows what happened to Zofia, really. If she was running, like Rivcze said, all over the woods looking for us, what do I have to risk? Here I know I'm going right to the death camp. Pregnant, I'm dead right away. At least for one night Zofia is going to let me in — if for two weeks she kept Rivcze with a retarded child and a cuckoo husband, why shouldn't she let me in at least for one night — what do I have to risk, right? So they said, yes, you are right, we have nothing to lose. And my grandmother said the same thing. Grandmother was still there, and the grandfather too — but they couldn't help it, they were old people, they had to wait for the deportation.

Israel

Frania's grandmother came to me, put her hands on me and cried. She said, "Israel, could you make a bunker for me and my husband?" I said, "I'll try." I knocked half a wall out from her room and I made the room smaller and built another wall. Then I made a wardrobe with a false back so you could get into that small room. I worked quite a long time on it, but I built it.

Frania

Before I left, my grandmother gave me a bottle of alcohol, a vodka — in Poland the vodka was 96%, very strong. When you have to give birth, at that time it's very important to have vodka — that's what my grandmother told me. I didn't know, I was so naïve. "But," she said, "don't show this to the farmer. Watch out for this like your own head, because you'll need it." That saved my life, that bottle. So I listened to my grandmother — she was an elderly woman — I really saved it. If I would give it to the farmer, I wouldn't have it, he would right away drink it. I saved it, all the time, because I knew in one month I have to give birth.

My grandmother, you know, before the war, she never gave me ten cents. I don't remember once receiving something, a gift from my grandmother. She told me the sun would shine when I got married — as long as it didn't cost her any money she could say everything. But listen, with her hands she gave me the alcohol, and maybe this saved my life.

Israel

Later on, after the war, we heard that Frania's grandfather died from hunger in a camp somewhere, we didn't know where. That's all that we heard about them. They were caught, that's for sure. Itchele and his son Leibick went to a farm to be hidden. Six months before the war finished, the farmer killed them.

Frania

My uncle Itchele had a very, very trusted farmer — the father of that young fellow who went by bicycle to Zofia. That farmer, an older man, brought a horse and a wagon with hay — and Israel was buried in the hay, under the straw. And he dressed me like a farmer's wife: he brought me a big, full skirt of his wife's — a stomach I had anyway — and a wool shawl, a dark green, I remember, for my head. I looked exactly like his wife, sitting together with him in the front, and Israel was under the straw.

We left five o'clock in the morning, November the fifth, 1942. And November the sixth, they took all the Jews out from Dzialoszyce — one day more would be too late. It was already cold, it was raining. The roads were so bad, and so bumpy, the farmer took two big towels, and he made a knot, and he said to me, "My child, put it around your stomach, because the roads are so bumpy, and it's very dangerous." And he did it by himself — I wasn't even shy — he put that towel around me. The farmer said, "I'm not going to sneak on the side ways. I'm going to go with the main roads." By the main roads you had to go through Pinczow by the main street where all the Gestapo were going — through there he went. Just like he's not afraid, he's a farmer, that's all. Can you imagine my heart? — and Israel was under the straw. We went right through Busko, and I saw all the Gestapo. I knew them, I recognized the faces, because they used to come to Pinczow all the time — I knew them very well. We went right through Pinczow to the village of Wlochy, three kilometres away. Outside the village there was a hill, and a big, big field, and there was one little house — Ludwig's. Half a mile away, another little house. He was separate, and that was the good thing about it, that he wasn't together with a neighbour next door.

Israel

We didn't know how they will receive us. Will they take us or not?

Frania

It was already pitch dark, when we got there. Zofia came out, and when she saw me and Israel, the way she grabbed me around, I could swear that a mother does not greet her own child the way she greeted me.

Israel

I got off the wagon and I saw Ludwig. I was more than a little bit scared because he had a stone face. He didn't smile, didn't say anything. Nothing.

Frania

Zofia told me that the week before she *did* come to Dzialoazyce. She got there, she asked where the post office is, people recognized right away that she is not from Dzialoszyce — you know, it's a very small place — and they said, "You come here for a Jew, or something like that? You better go home, because the Germans will suspect that you come for the Jews, they'll shoot you right here." Listen, how should she know? She was afraid. She came into Dzialoszyce but she didn't even get as far as the post office – the minute she came, she went right back. She got cold feet. But she came. By foot, she came. Imagine. So I was right, that we went to her.

Israel

I'll tell you what I thought – even though now it's embarrassing for me. I was considering that Zofia didn't run to Dzialoszyce to save us for the sake of saving us, she came because she knew that the flour mill is ours, and later she's going to get a lot of money out of us. A day after we came, she asks, "How much money do you have?" But the real truth is, she had heart.

Frania

Zofia was kissing me, and she started to cross herself, like the Messiah was born, how happy she was to see us. So I was right: what do I have to lose, why do I have to go to deportation right away? A day is a day. I don't know what's going to be tomorrow. I said to myself: I'm going to survive this war.

Part Three

Ludwig and Zofia lived there in a small wooden house. They had a young boy, Maniek, he was seven years old. Later we found out the boy was not Ludwig's — it was her child from someone else. The house was divided in two: half was a stable and in the other half they lived, in one room. They didn't have a slice of bread there. A mouse in a church is poor? That's the way they were poor — they had nothing. Nothing. Ludwig didn't even have a horse for the field. Naturally, we came right away with money, and then later we said we're going to be in contact with the rest of our family for more money — but I didn't believe that myself. In Dzialoszyce there was a telephone, at least I could still call — but here? I didn't know what happened to my father, to anybody. We came to Ludwig so ripped away from everything familiar, we didn't know a thing. But you know what? I believe very much in fate. It was just meant in heaven that we should survive that war. Because everything was going with such a coincidence for us to be alive. I can see that now. How should I know if I'll see my family? My sisters went to Warsaw, how should I know where? Where will I write? How should they know where Ludwig is? And coincidence happened that I knew right away after one week where they are. That's a storybook. I'm telling you, it's a storybook of miracles.

I told you my grandmother gave me the bottle of vodka. That alcohol I was hiding. But she also gave me two beautiful loaves of white bread. Right away we took that out, and naturally they ate it with us, and their little boy shared it too.

Ludwig said that first he wants my baby to be born, before he lets us stay in the house. First he wants us to be in the hayloft. We had some money, so naturally we gave them some right away. They didn't even talk about money first, because Zofia was so happy to see us, I just can't tell you. Ludwig was not cold, and not hot. He didn't have anything, so he figured we will give him some money. He was afraid, so afraid. I don't blame him.

We wanted a good watch-dog. So we gave sixty zlotys to Ludwig, and he went to town. Israel told him to go to Mr Roit. He had terrific dogs. This was the same Mr Roit that gave us the room for the dancing, years before when we first met. Of course, Mr Roit went with the deportation but we were sure somebody lives there in his house, and has his dogs. He had such well-trained dogs, that you've never seen in your life. Ludwig should buy a dog from these people. We wanted to have a good watch-dog, if somebody comes suddenly, we should have a warning.

So Ludwig went into Pinczow, and he bought a black dog. He was beautiful. And he had above his eyes two gold-coloured dots, so we gave him a name, Kropka. In English this means "a dot." Kropka saved our life many, many times. He was so smart. When it came night, and we went out a little bit in the fresh air, we knew that a mile away from far, Kropka could smell already if somebody was coming, and he would start to bark. So we could sit outside, a little fresh air to have, you see. Kropka knew that we come out only at night. He knew that in the daytime they locked the door, they go to work in the field, and we are left inside. He had outside a dog house, he was sitting on top, like a prince. In the daytime I would look at him through the window, he would look back at me and wag his tail, flirting with me. I'm telling you, it was amazing how this dog was smart. He knew that he has to watch us. We took him at night — let's say, eleven o'clock — we went out for a walk, and we took a rope — the rope must have been two, three hundred feet long — and he ran in the field before us. But the minute he felt that a stranger is near, he came running back, and he pulled us to the house. You've never seen such a smart dog.

Ludwig had two sisters in Warsaw. One sister, her name was Wichta, was a nothing. She was an ugly old maid, a rotten character. The other sister, her name was Juzia, was the nicest person. She had a boy in that time of seven, eight years. Her husband was working in a post office in Warsaw, but he made so little that it wasn't enough for the family, so she was coming to Pinczow to buy butter, geese, ham — different things — she smuggled it back to Warsaw, and sold it there on the black market. That way she made money. She came every week like this. Zofia came up to our hayloft there and told us that Ludwig will tell his sisters about us, but not yet — in the meantime he doesn't want to say anything. We will wait another week, let's see what's going to happen. We have to tell them, because if they're coming here, they stay two, three days — and they're going to find out anyway — we have to tell them.

Every Tuesday and Friday was market day, and when they came again the following week, they were told about us. And we met. Zofia introduced us to them, because at night we used to come down from the loft to stretch our legs. We had supper down there and then later we walked around a little bit. We went up again at night, when everything already was quiet. Anyway, she introduced us to them, and we told a little bit of the story about what happened to the family.

So Juzia says, "Do you have a sister named Zosha?" I'm telling you, the minute she told me, I had a feeling....

"I think," she said, "that your sisters live in my house."

I said, "What do you mean, Juzia?"

She says, "You want to know, I could swear, the way you're telling me stories, that your sisters live with me in my house."

How come? Because life is so hard, her husband doesn't make enough, they decided to rent a room. Where they lived, there was a big doorway to the street and through that door was a big yard with lots of apartments around. So there, in order to rent a room, or sell something, you put out a little ticket on that street door, and people passing on the street read it, like in a newspaper. So when Shaindele came to Warsaw, she needed somewhere to go, so she went around different streets and she looked up these addresses, and it just happened she found this one — of Juzia, Ludwig's sister. What do you say to this coincidence?

She went in there — she didn't say she is Jewish, nothing — and said that she wants to rent a room. Juzia rented to her, and she didn't suspect Shaindele of being Jewish. But later she suspected Malkale. First came Shaindele by herself, but when Malkale came, Juzia saw already that they're not Gentiles.

Shaindele realized that Juzia is a nice woman, and her husband is an angel, such a good man, so — you've got to have somebody to talk to, you had to trust somebody — Shaindele told them everything.

Well, when Juzia came, and she saw that Ludwig had us, and we started to talk a little bit, and tell stories about family, she said, "I could swear that these are your sisters." I didn't know the names they had on the passports: Shaindele made her name "Zosha," and Malkale on the passport was "Marisha." So she started to tell me what they look like, and I said, "That's it."

Juzia went back and she told Shaindele and Malkale, and they said, "Sure, that's them."

Can you imagine, a coincidence like this? If not this, we could never survive, because we didn't have enough money, and Shaindele was sending it to us every week with Yusza.

Chamel gave all the money, a bag with gold, to Shaindele. He said, "You have to have it, because if any one of us lives, I'm sure you're going to be the one, because you don't look Jewish at all — nobody would have even the guts and the nerve to accuse you."

The Gentiles were walking in Warsaw on the streets and by the look in the eyes they recognized a Jew, and they used blackmail. They did it once with my sisters. Shaindele took Malkale once for a walk, and two Poles walked right over to her, and said, "You better give me six hundred zlotys because you are hiding here a Jewish girl" — they meant Malkale. "You're hiding her, you better pay for it. Otherwise…" She paid.

And they didn't go home a whole day, they were watching if the Poles would follow her home, because if they would know where she lives, they would come every day.

My sisters later moved out of Juzia's — it wasn't too convenient, it was small — but Shaindele still gave her the money for us, and letters, and everything. They rented from another woman, a widow. Nobody knew they were Jews. Malkale always stayed indoors because of that blackmailing incident. Shaindele told this widow that Malkale is a sick girl, and she has to take so many pills, that she's got some blood disease. Shaindele was buying pills, and throwing them to the toilet. She was afraid to let Malkale go to work.

But Shaindele went to work because she didn't want the widow to be suspicious. The money she made from work — I think in a variety-type store — she didn't need because she had all the gold from Chamel.

So there was an old bachelor, a Jew from Pinczow — his name was Felix — he was hidden by Poles in Warsaw. He had no money at all — before the war he was such a rich man — he had to keep changing places to hide every few weeks.

So Shaindele always met Felix on the street alone and gave him *all* the money she made from that job.

Shaindele was sending us money every week with Juzia, you could trust her. And the letters too, she sent with Juzia. And she sent us papers to read, and books. So Ludwig knew that we haven't got all the money with us. That would be dangerous for us — who knew what he could be capable of doing. He knew the money comes from Warsaw, from my sisters.

I remember that Shaindele told us they bought flower pots, and all the gold was hidden there in the soil. And later on when it was an alarm — they were bombarding Warsaw — they used to go to the public bunker, and they had to grab out that gold because they never knew what's going to happen.

She wrote once in a letter: "We have to accept that something could happen — it's a war — that Juzia won't be able to travel any more, and we're not going to have a way to send you money. And if you're going to be left without money, Ludwig could throw you out. We have to think about it, that it could happen."

She was right — it did happen. In 1944, the Germans rounded up young Polish men and women and took them to work in ammunition factories in Berlin. So the Germans took in that time Shaindele and Malkale, too, as Gentiles. She didn't have much gold left but she took it with her. Right before that happened Shaindele sent us a book and between the pages she put some money. Nobody knew we had it. We kept it for insurance. And you know what happened? Ludwig was better to us in the last six months, without money, than he was when we gave him the money. He wanted to show us that he is a sport. He was such a funny man, you could never reach this man, what kind of a character he was. He wanted to show us that he could be so nice to us without money, better than with money — he was such a character. So when we were liberated, we still had the money left in the book — because later already we were afraid to show him the money — he'll think we have even more. And then he could kill us, you understand?

When I had to give birth, it was December the twenty-second, just before Christmas. I came to the farm in November, so I was there already seven weeks. In the beginning Juzia was coming twice a week for market days. Twice a week she and her sister Wichta were smuggling at that time because it was before Christmas, so they bought a lot of the geese, butter, and whatever would be in short supply in Warsaw. The whole month Shaindele was sending absorbent cotton, and flash-lights — I could have made a store. Why did she send so much? I should have the cotton for the bleeding; and she was sending the flashlights because if I'm going to give birth, it has to be lit up, and Ludwig said never is he going to allow us to put candles there. I don't blame him. The roof on that hayloft was made of pieces of wood and straw on top. We could all go up in fire. To

vi Zev Rubinek, Israel's father.

Israel's mother, Sarah (Zawadzki) Rubinek,
who died just after he was born.

rael's grandfather, Rabbi Michael Zawadzki, with his wife Miriam.

Frania's school photograph, Pinczow, 1926,
when she was six years old.

Frania and her youngest brother, Yossele, taken
just before the war.

Srulcie, Frania's brother.

Chamel, Frania's oldest brother.

Frania's father, Shloime-Baruch Greenfeld.

square in Pinczow, before the war.

burned-out remains of the square after the German invasion.

These photographs were taken the day the Jews of Pinczow were rounded up for deportation.

Hadas Rubinek, Israel's aunt.

Frania's sisters Malkale (left) and Shaindele (right) while living
in Warsaw as Gentiles. They are carrying Bibles and are on
their way to church. The men in the background are German
soldiers.

Frania and Israel in 1947

In the Displaced Persons camp, Föhrenwald.

Zofia and Ludwig Banya, after the war, circa 1950.

Israel performing in *Gold Diggers* by Sholom Aleichem, in Föhrenwald.

Israel performs the title role (on stilts), of the Golem, by H. Leivick in Föhrenwald.

Israel and Jacob Sandler, co-directors of the theatre company in Föhrenwald.

Ludwig and Frania in Lodz, circa 1945.

Saul, 8 months old, with Israel, in the Displaced Persons camp.

Frania and 18-month old Saul, in Montreal, 1950.

The Rubinek family, 1952, in Montreal.

go in the house, he was afraid, Ludwig. And he was thinking what to do with the child. Anyway, it was set up that Juzia should take the child, and to wait, let's say, a few days, and after a few days she'll bring it to Warsaw, they're going to give it there to the nuns. People did that a lot, and they are still looking for the children today. And how many children they don't even know who they are? You read the stories — I don't know if you did — but I read plenty of stories. The point is we wrote about this arrangement to Shaindele, but we didn't tell Ludwig or Zofia nothing. Maybe we should have told her, but listen, I'm not going to cry over spilt milk. If not Zofia, I wouldn't be sitting here, of that you could be sure.

I went to Pinczow one night, with her. Imagine — by foot, and with my stomach. I dressed like a farmer-woman and we went at night, when nobody could recognize me. I went there to a Gentile woman who used to be a customer of ours in the store. I knew that my mother gave away to this woman blankets, pillows, tablecloths. I remembered a down comforter — I wanted to get that, because where we were hiding it was so freezing cold. I figured, maybe she'll give me something back. She gave me — not everything, but she was a very nice woman — I wouldn't go if I wouldn't know she's nice. She gave me three, four pillows, and she gave me that down comforter — and this saved my life, because it was so cold. When we curled up under this, we were warm — otherwise with what could you cover yourself in that hayloft? Zofia carried it on her back, and we went like this home — it was already two o'clock in the morning.

When it came the day for me to give birth, it was cold — thirty below. I had a grey coat — I'll never forget it — a winter coat, flannel, with black seal lapels. And I had high leather boots, they were in style at that time — and like this I gave birth. Israel was the doctor, with Zofia.

You know, they put flashlights into the straw, and they tied my mouth with a towel, I shouldn't be able to yell. And the child got born, and I heard crying. So Israel got old that night, because even today, if he sees blood, he could faint — but what could he do? After the baby was born comes the afterbirth, so he didn't even know what it is. Naturally, we were very naïve — what do you think, Poland is like here? — children know now everything. Israel said to me, "Frania, it's still coming something." So I said, "If it's coming, take. What do I know?" And the child was born, but Israel didn't know how to cut the cord. I think Zofia knew, but she didn't want to do it. I'm sure she knew, because when she had Maniek, she gave birth to him in the field, and she did everything herself. Well, she said she doesn't know what to do. Israel really didn't know what to do. But what Zofia thought and what she knew or not, it's not fair for me to say. Maybe it's for the better. Listen, there is a tree, there are branches — as you see, I had another child. Anyway, the child was overcome with blood, because they didn't cut the cord, so naturally, the child died, and Zofia buried it.

In the meantime, I was very sick, because when Israel saw a little head, he had to pull fast, so he tore me probably in six places — and how can you heal this? And this was burning and hurting. Zofia said there is a herb you brew like tea, and from this it's going to be good to make compresses. First of all, I was bleeding a terrible amount. All right, I had a lot of absorbent cotton, that was good, but later you had to bury it somewhere. Zofia did it, and Israel, they went down at night, and buried it outside. But this torn place was burning, terrible. Terrible aches. You see, I just couldn't take it. Zofia brewed that tea in the house, and she brought it up. Israel put compresses on all the time, to heal. So it healed like this, and it was never sewn together, you understand. When I came to Canada years after, the doctor in Montreal said he doesn't have to do nothing, it's okay.

After three, four days, the milk starts to get into your breasts. You have to do something about this too, you understand. Okay, so on the right side, it went away by itself, but the left side…what happened? Ludwig came up, he said he just came from the village, they say the Germans are going to look for the Jews again. Israel said we have to hide under the straw, and our down comforter had to be taken downstairs, they shouldn't see anything. It was dark up there, it was at night. Israel wanted to lie down and he didn't know that I sat up too — with his elbow he went right into my breast. And I had there the milk, after the third, fourth day. Was I sick. On that breast, he gave me a knock — oh! I was so sick, that I was already dying. Dying. You know what, I was lying there, and Israel touched me everywhere, my feet, my fingers, my body, everything was just stopped, numb. I didn't feel anything — all the body was dead already. But my mind — I heard, I understood everything when they talked to each other, but I couldn't answer. I remember Zofia came up, and she said to him, "Israel, she's dying, you could see she is dying." Israel was hanging over me, and he was crying. I couldn't say a word. My senses I had, that's all: I could see, but I couldn't move. So she said to him, "Israel, you see she's dying. There is one thing: if she's strong, if she's got a strong heart, one thing we could do. Have you got alcohol?" She knew about it, you see. "Give me the alcohol. I have pepper downstairs, I'm going to chop it up — and this, with the alcohol, is going to burn through her fever, if she is strong enough. She'll sleep two days, but she'll make it. And she is dying anyway, you cannot do anything, we have to take that chance." So what could he do, Israel? He saw that I'm dying. He said, "All right." They gave it to me to drink, and I didn't feel — to me it was just like I would drink water. I fell asleep, and I slept three days. Israel was over me, always, listening if I'm breathing. As long as I breathe, he let me alone. After that, when I woke up, I felt already everything, but I was weak. I was past the crisis. Everything burned through, like she said, Zofia. Was I sick — I couldn't even lift a hand. She was cooking for me, that time, such soups, and a lot of the butter she didn't take to the market, she gave to me.

Then started the story with my breast. Started to get boils, and the pains were so terrible that I would bite my finger through to blood. I couldn't cry, I couldn't yell, I couldn't scream. And this was going on like this for three months. And you couldn't go to a drugstore to buy something. Once Zofia came, and she said that she has got a leaf, if you put this leaf on the boils, it heals. So what did I have to risk? I used the leaf, and you know what the leaf did? It ate away a piece of my skin. And I still have a mark there from that. It ate away, it made a hole, from that leaf. I was in pain for three months. And after that, all these boils burst, and the pus was just running out. After the war, I went to a doctor, and when he asked me about my history, I told him about this and he said it's unbelievable. To have a child born when you don't know what to do, and not to have an infection? And later this infection in my breast, and to live? This is unbelievable. We lived in that barn the whole winter. After I took sick, and after I had my child, we finally came down into the house.

∽ ISRAEL ∾

Once in the middle of the night, the dog started to bark. I wasn't sleeping — I hardly slept there for two and a half years — I was always looking out the window, if somebody is coming. The dog started to bark, I looked out, I saw someone, just a silhouette. Outside was a boy, and calling, 'Israel! Israel! Help me! Help me! I know you are there. I haven't got where to go."

We recognized the voice, it was a cousin of ours. I wanted to let him in.

Ludwig stood up and said, "If you're going to tell him that you are here, I'll let you all go out and never come back. You just sit, and don't answer."

And it was just heartbreaking. He was sixteen years old.

He started to yell, "Israel, Israel, help me, help me!" He stood there and he was yelling, that boy, for probably half an hour. We cried, and we begged Ludwig and nothing helped.

Later on we heard that some farmers took him in for a little while but soon threw him out. He went to another city and became a servant to the Germans. You know what he did? When the Germans were hunting, they used him to retrieve the dead rabbits. Instead of a dog, they used him. He was blond and the Germans didn't know he's Jewish. Now, he is alive, he's in Israel and has two sons in the Israeli Air Force. We saw him after the war and he had nothing against us, he understood perfectly. He wasn't sure at that time we were at the farm — somebody told him that probably Rubinek and the Greenfeld girl are hidden at Ludwig's. He was my uncle's cousin. The relation is not important, even if it would be a stranger, I would let him in — but I couldn't.

⌒ FRANIA ⌒

All day we stayed in the house. Israel was sitting at the window, and the dog was outside watching. The first little while we were there, Israel slept on the floor for a few hours at night, but later he was sitting at the window to watch, because he was afraid the dog could fall asleep. And when he finally slept he would sleep beside the little boy, Maniek, on a bag of straw.

They had there an oven for wood. There was a little opening where she baked her own bread — every two weeks, twice a month. That oven was the whole wall, till the ceiling, and then there was a little opening on top, a yard by a yard. I put a little sack there, filled with straw. That was my bedroom. I never felt so good as when I went there at night, even though I couldn't stretch. Ludwig and Zofia had their bed almost right underneath, so, you know, everything I saw, and everything I heard. Well, how could you help it? When I stretched my legs, they would stick out and he would yell at me because it was almost in their bed. But I was afraid that my legs would be so cramped, I wouldn't be able to stretch any more. After all, we were there twenty-eight months. It's not a day, twenty-eight months.

On the side of the stove near the floor was a door that went to a cellar. That little cellar was exactly as big as where I was sleeping — a yard by a yard. She had the potatoes there. Israel made two little chairs — we put the potatoes to the side — and the minute we thought somebody's coming, we opened that little door, and slid down. My knees were always bleeding, and Israel, his trousers had one patch on top of the other, from sliding down to that little cellar. Usually, the little boy, Maniek, or Ludwig had to run fast and close it. But later Israel made two handles on the bottom, he pulled it to himself and closed it right away. We could sometimes sit there for hours — because once in a while farmers came to visit on a Sunday. If they came suddenly, we had to run to the cellar, but if we knew that they're coming, we went into the barn, and up to that little hayloft. There we could be more comfortable than the cellar where you couldn't even cough. It was very hard to sit there, specially in the cold wintertime, and in the summertime it was very stuffy. So like this it wasn't good, and like that it wasn't good. But what could you do? Sometimes they came, the farmers, and they sat for hours with their stories that weren't worth a single cent — but we had to sit there.

Ludwig was a very common man. He told us once a story, I don't know if it's true, but Israel said that he could believe it, Ludwig was so cold-blooded — somebody who could kill and not even give a wink with an eye, such a man he was. He told us that once he worked in a factory in Warsaw, where there were big ovens. There was a man working with them they didn't like — so during the night they put him inside that oven, and they burned him. Israel said he could believe it — such a type he was, Ludwig.

~~ ISRAEL ~~

Ludwig was thirty-six years old when we came to him. Five feet, eight inches tall, thin, a face with no expression at all. Only when he ate, he smiled — he never laughed with his whole heart, he only smiled. When he got up in the morning, the first thing he did was kneel down to the picture of Mary, scratched his back, and right away he started to yell at his wife — this was five in the morning — in five seconds the prayer was done. I was sitting at the table, still up from a whole night of watching out the window, and I looked at him with wonder, what kind of people are in this world. After his five-second prayer he started to yell at Zofia to get up right away, and if she didn't, he'd throw a wooden shoe at her. She got up. Right away she would take her kerchief and she would cover her mouth — that meant she was mad. And he used to be mad if anything got in his way. I was sitting in my corner not moving even — like a fly scared to fly — so mad he was. And she jumped down from bed, and made right away potatoes with borscht. When he was eating, he was sitting at the table with a spoon, looking straight into the plate, not taking away his eyes for a second — and sweat came on his face, and ran from his face right into the plate and he still didn't move — until he finished, and then he started to smile.

Then he walked over to us, and we were looking out like dogs from the hiding place in the cellar. He looked down and I looked up to him, and he asked, "Would you like a little potatoes?" "Yes." "Would you like a little bit more?" He was always teasing: what is a Jew? A Jew is nothing. They're not human. Everybody can kill them. I can't kill a dog, but if I'll kill you, I can always get some money for you. It's nothing." We are nothings.

Ludwig practically didn't have even what to eat. His farming was very poor. We gave Ludwig money — but slowly. We got scared if he will know that we have some money with us, he would kill us. Just the same, I was prepared, because I got a hunting knife with me. Ludwig used to buy leaves of tobacco, and I sharpened a knife, very sharp, and at night-time I sat down to cut tobacco from the leaves for him for the next day, and for myself. I was always thinking: maybe Ludwig will want to kill us, I wouldn't let him. I'll kill him first. I always had my knife with me. We were living from minute to minute. We didn't know the next day if we would be alive. Once, I was down hidden in the cellar, I heard him talking to his wife: he is sick and tired of the Jews, he has sharp axes, he will cut off our heads, and show them to the Germans — and for that he would get two kilograms of sugar. I was looking for ways to show him I would not go so easy — that I'm stronger than he thinks I am.

The farmers were ordered to cut down trees and bring them to the Germans, but they stole a little bit for themselves too, to have wood for the winter. Ludwig had a lot of those trees in his yard. One time, Zofia told Ludwig that she heard the man who looks after the forest is going to every farmer and seeing how many trees had been stolen by the workers. So we had to hide those trees. A tree has a thin side and a thick side, and he told me to go to the thin side, because he was considering himself very strong. I picked up my side, but he couldn't pick up his. I told him that he is not so strong like I am. I said let him go to the thin side and I'll go by myself to the thick side. I picked up the thick side better than him. I did it special with all my strength to show him that I'm stronger than him. He looked at me, "Oh, I didn't know that you were so strong."

Once, in the spring of '43, he came in the house busting with laughter — so I knew that something is not right. He said he was at the Pinczow market and the Germans caught a Jew named Herschkowic — I knew him. Ludwig said the Jew was begging the Germans not to kill him, and they asked him to show where he was hiding his money. After he showed it to them, they killed him. Ludwig thought it was funny: "That stupid Jew, why did he show where the money is?" I was so mad, I said, "I'm not going to beg. If Gestapo comes in here, I will be on top of him with my knife." I grabbed Ludwig with all my power, I nearly squeezed him, I said, "Just like this I'm going to do it. I'm going to kill right away — before he takes out his revolver, I'll be on him with my knife." And I won a little bit of respect from him.

Ludwig used to come back six or seven o'clock at night — he never came home for lunch, he took something to eat with him — when he came home at night, he sat down at the table, put his head in his hands and was sitting and not moving for hours, till Zofia made supper. When she made supper — it was usually noodles — it had to be the right amount because he always put his spoon into the plate of food and if the spoon stood up and didn't fall, he was happy. He ate the same way as in the morning — when he finished, he smiled. Later he used to whittle wood, whatever he needed around the farm — like sticks in the garden for a fence. He used to show off what he made and told me that a Jew cannot make that. So I made a bin you put corn into for the chickens to eat. He didn't want to believe it — he was so mad. He was scared to put it out into the yard, because people would wonder where he had the time to do that. Also, he was spitting on the floor, and that was disgusting, so I made a wooden spittoon for him. I hollowed out a piece of wood with four legs and I put sand in it and he had it near his bed.

Sometimes he would come from the market with a newspaper. I was anxious to read it, but he kept the paper in his hands, not reading, till he sat down to eat. He hardly could read, and what he read he didn't understand. After an hour, he just threw it to me, like to a dog. He asked me always, "Now, tell me what they're writing." The truth is, I only told him about what they were writing that was good for me: that the Russians were winning, no matter what was happening really. But the paper was German controlled, and never wrote that the Russians were leading. I used to tell him the truth is that the Russians pushed the Germans back, but they couldn't write that — they had to write, "They pulled back, for strategic reasons." And he understood me. Actually, I believed it too,

that way. But my main point was that he should believe that
the Russians are always nearer and nearer.

Sunday, the farmers came together at Ludwig's, and they
used to say, "Hey, Ludwig, you know the politics the best, tell
us." So he just used to repeat like a gramophone what I told
him. He became for them the smartest in the village. Once, he
was telling them about politics, and I heard how the farmers
said, "Oh, Churchill says it's a good thing the Germans and the
Russians should hit each other, and we will come in the
middle, hit them both, and we will take Poland back." It was
just a joke — it was to laugh, how they were talking.

Sometimes, they would get together on Sunday, what they
talked wasn't so funny. Some of them said the only good thing
Hitler did is kill the Jews — that's the first thing. They talked
like this: "There was a Jew with a corner grocery store. I liked
to buy from him, because he always asked me about how my
cows are, my chickens, how's my wife. And I brought him
some onions, beans — he was a nice Jew, they shouldn't kill
him. The others — I wouldn't care, but him they should leave."
Only that Jew they should leave because he was asking how's
his cow and his wife. Another farmer said: "There's another
Jew that has a grocery store. You see, I'm going into the
Catholic stores and I have to take off my hat — I have to stand
like I would be a nobody. But when I'm coming into that Jew's
grocery store, I am at home, I don't have to take off my hat. I'm
talking to him, and sometimes if I'm buying, he says, 'For that?
Twenty groschen.' If I give him only seventeen groschen,
sometimes he takes it. But in a Catholic store, when they say
twenty groschen — oh no, I have to pay twenty groschen, and
stand with my hat off. Those few Jews they should let live. I
would like that." Another said: "Oh, what are you talking. It's
the best thing that Hitler kills all the Jews. They killed Lord
Jesus Christ, they should be killed."

We seldom talked to Ludwig. When I wanted to ask him
something, he was always mad, because he considered us a

nuisance. He used to consider a Jew as just a waste, not worth bothering about, just an animal. He only talked to me when he wanted something from me.

In the mornings, he started to walk around and look for his axes, but the axes were hidden. Every night Frania hid them in a new place because she got scared when he comes home at night, he'll cut our heads off. He was cursing, looking for his axes and cursing. He couldn't talk good Polish, so he couldn't even swear with the right pronunciation. Finally he'd find them — sometimes under a cushion, or in the stable, just where he wouldn't have it handy. He took the axes, his saw, and went to the woods to work. When he walked out, we could breathe a little bit easier.

Frania

Once Ludwig said to Zofia — and I heard it myself — he was fed up with us, it was taking too long. And you know, when the dog started to bark that someone's coming, you saw that he was afraid — you just saw all his blood coming down out of his face. Because if they would catch us in this place, they would kill him with us together.

Israel

When Ludwig and his wife were good to each other, it was very bad for us. At the beginning, when they started to fight between themselves, we got scared, and I tried to make peace between them. But it turned out whenever they fought, each was good to us, each gave us to eat. She had a babushka over her head, and when she put it over her mouth, we knew that they were were mad at each other. Then they both were good to us: we should eat — they gave us the first portion — everything the best.

When they were good to each other, they forgot us, and didn't give us to eat. They just made us miserable. How? Everything we did, wasn't good. And they're afraid that over us they're going to be killed — you know, they nag, nag, nag, and they made us miserable, that's all, period.

Frania

They were fighting over things, it was ridiculous, a comedy, you could make theatre out of it. For example, he would say to her that she came with no dowry. You see, for them to have a decent plate, or just a spoon, was a fortune. When I brought there some pillows, and that down comforter, this was like getting, I don't know, a hundred thousand dollars or something. So he said, "You came to me with what? With a bastard, and with a naked behind." When he took her, she already had Maniek. She worked as a maid probably in a big mansion for a landowner — probably she had his child, because Maniek looked so delicate and nice — and a heart! — you could look at his face, you could see that he comes from a better kind of people. So she said, "What? You're going to tell me that I came with nothing? I brought here the *cebzik*." And what is a *cebzik*? There wasn't a bathroom to wash — where did you wash? There was a barrel and this was called a *cebzik*. It was made from wood, and all around it was iron, holding it — thirty inches around, with two handles. And in this you wash the dishes, in this you washed yourself — took me time to get used to it, but listen, I wanted to be clean, I had to get used to it — Ludwig washed his legs in that, I washed my body, my hair, later we washed the dishes, everything was in that *cebzik*. All of us, all five of us.

Israel

Ludwig went to wash himself, he took his two hands with a little bit of water, threw it on his face, and that's it — washed.

Frania

Zofia said, "I came with nothing?! I brought you that *cebzik*. And I brought two spoons! How would you eat if you wouldn't have the two spoons I brought you? And what do you think, to who are you praying? To my picture! This picture of the virgin Maria is my picture!" Honestly, this picture, you couldn't even see if there's a Maria there — it was all faded away. She said, "You could pray if you didn't have my picture?!" So he didn't know what to answer, she really brought the *cebzik* and she brought the picture. She brought the two spoons. But he said, "I gave you the house, you wouldn't even have nothing over your head if I didn't have that house. Where would you be?" That house: the floors weren't made of wood — the richer ones, they had it — but the majority of the farmers where I was around Pinczow, nobody had it. There was just earth. They were bringing in everything from the yard, so I swept with a broom they had — and the broom wasn't a broom like you have here, but it was made by themselves — I swept a little bit that earth, because always it was filthy. I took some yellow sand — they were buying it or getting it, I don't know from where — and I spread it around a little bit, so it looked a little nice. Some house.

Israel

He hit her once in the mouth — with his foot. She was passing him down the hay, and she didn't do it right, he didn't catch it. So he came up to her, and hit her with the foot to the mouth, and made a swollen mouth.

Ludwig himself was a sadist. He told me once, he got a dog, and put a rope to his neck, and put him down in the well, and he was pulling him up and down in the well, till he was dead. Such a sadist was he.

Ludwig did never like the boy. He used to kick Maniek around. The boy liked me very much. As a matter of fact, at night-time when he came home from school, I taught him how to read and how to write. They had the books, the Catholic prayer books, so I taught him also the

Catholic catechism, how to say the prayers. The boy liked me very, very much — and Ludwig always kicked him. Maniek was very handsome and very good and very understanding. He was told by his mother that if somebody asked him anything, not to say, because if he will say something, Mr and Mrs Rubinek will get killed. He didn't want that. So he kept his mouth shut and never opened it for anybody, not even his friends. He was very smart and reliable.

Frania

You know, one time Ludwig and Zofia were away in town, and Israel wanted once to have a little sleep so he said to the boy, "Maniek, you're going out to play, but if you'll see somebody's coming, wake me up because I want to sleep a little bit. Frania is going to do the washing, so she is going to be busy." He said all right.

All of a sudden, I go to the window, just to give a look, and I see Maniek waves with his hand, slow — he was only seven years old — and he kept his hand low. I didn't know what he meant, so I woke up Israel, I said, "Something is wrong — Maniek is making a sign." Israel said, "I think if Maniek is not running, it's probably nothing but I don't know, let's go first to the cellar." We ran into that little cellar, and sure enough, a woman came, with a boy, she was looking for somebody.

Later, when she left, Maniek said, "You see, I am not stupid. I saw them coming. I know they're coming to visit my parents. If I would run, they will think right away: 'Oh, Maniek is running — somebody is there hidden.'"

Israel

Zofia was a very small woman, very hard-working. And she was a woman of good nature. If we wanted something, we always asked her, when he wasn't at home. She was the same age as Ludwig. She suffered a lot — he treated her very badly. We always had pity for her.

Across the road, nearly a half a mile away, was a neighbour — her name was Dzubinska, and she was so nosy, she always wanted to know everything. She was a typical peasant woman, big, fat, and walked fast. And always, when she was talking she kept her hands under her apron, with her thumbs under her fingers and that was so nobody could give her the evil eye. Superstitious. And always, she came in suddenly. She wanted to see what they're eating, always. But no matter how suddenly she came, I always saw her before. We had to hide everything right away when she came in — the meat, the noodles — because none of the farmers around could afford those things. Not far from us, was living a widow woman, and she was hiding also a Jew. Zofia went for something to borrow, she saw him, and she came back and told us. But that widow woman was such a Cossack, she wasn't scared of anybody. She was so fierce that she could kill even a policeman. The people in the village even got scared of her. She had two sons and she told them not to tell anybody and nobody opened the mouth. Zofia knew he was a Jew when she saw him because she recognized him — his grandfather had a grocery store that they used to go to. The widow knew that Zofia wouldn't talk because they assumed that Ludwig also has somebody hidden. People didn't know for sure, but they talked vaguely. Actually they didn't believe it because there was no room at Ludwig's to hide somebody. The widow did it for money, and she thought the Jew was going to marry her. He was living quite a while with her after the war. But he couldn't marry her, he just couldn't. After the war, he went away with her, with the children and they opened a store near the German border, but he left her later with

the store with the money, with everything, and he went to
Israel.

Frania

The village was talking already, that Ludwig and Zofia are
hiding somebody. They saw already that they dressed a
little better. And we were watching out for this, but it's
hard, you know, it's hard. When they were eating the
noodles, that was a luxury. If they were eating this, if
somebody was coming, everything was right away thrown
in the oven — those things could give us away. But they
didn't see anything, they didn't see us. But people were
talking, that Ludwig is better off than he was before —
you know, they're suspecting already. Well, that's why
one farmer gave away the other. That's what was happening. We were just lucky, because we told them, if you're
going to show your neighbours that you are eating so
well, they'll know right away: before you didn't have even
a piece of bread.

Israel

One farmer came into the house in the middle of the week
and saw that Ludwig ate meat. He said, "Oh, Ludwig, did
you get rich? In the middle of the week you're eating meat?
We're eating meat only on Sunday. Oh, something is going
on here. Have you killed some Jews?" They were suspicious
but they weren't sure.

When they went Sunday to church, neighbours used to
come near the windows and to look in. I saw them
coming — the dog used to warn me.

Sometimes that woman Dzubinska wanted to borrow
the mill they had there and asked Ludwig to give the key,
when they're going to the church, she could come in, and
grind some wheat to make flour. When I heard that I understood she wanted to come in and to look around. The
entrance to the stable was from the outside, but you could

also go in from the kitchen, through a small door straight to the stable. We were standing there quiet, for four, five hours, and I closed the small door to the kitchen with a hook. But Dzubinska was ripping that door, trying to go into the house to look if somebody is there, but she couldn't.

I always was watching, so not to miss one single minute. It happened sometimes, sitting at the table and eating, you missed with your eyes to look out, or the dog fell asleep. And suddenly you hear the door opening and the dog gave out with a sudden wowowowowow. We had two seconds to jump into the hiding place, but we did it.

Frania

One night Ludwig came home, and said they're talking in the village that tonight they are going to come here, the Germans, and they are going to look for Jews, if somebody's not hidden in a bunker, or something. So at that time, we didn't have anything prepared. So where are we going to hide? The Germans would find the little cellar right away. So Israel said, "You know what, we're going to go into the oven." Listen, what can you do, we survive. He went in like nothing. My hips, you know I have trouble with my hips, I couldn't get in, I was too wide. So what shall I do? We have to hide. Israel said, "If you cannot get in, it's no use. I'll go outside, and the dog will start to bark, so that means the Germans are coming on the other side of the hill — so we'll still have time to run into the field. They're not going to look in the field, they're going to look just if there's a hiding place inside the house." It was in the wintertime, and it must have been thirty below, Poland was very cold. So he said he is going outside, and he didn't let me go with him because he knew when I go up to my place over the oven, I relax a little bit. I had so much migraine, and I was so sick, all the time, so he wanted me to relax there. He is going to go outside, and he was afraid the dog sometimes could fall asleep too —

you know, he's a live thing, he could fall asleep for a second. So he said, "I'm going to watch outside, together with the dog, and the minute the dog will bark, that somebody is coming, I'll take you, and we'll run to the field." Right away Ludwig crossed himself. Israel went out, and he used to come in every fifteen minutes, you know, to warm up a little bit. Ludwig and Zofia went to sleep. Then I didn't see him, I didn't see him. So I was sitting and sitting, I didn't see him − I woke up Zofia. I said, "Israel didn't come back. What happened? He wasn't here for an hour already." She went out, and she saw that he is all frozen. But he was already waking up, coming to his senses. He fell asleep, from the cold, and the dog − he was so smart, this dog − saw that he's already almost dead, so he started to rub him, and warm him, and he woke him up, the dog. And if not the dog, he would have frozen to death outside. Imagine. Anyway, the Germans didn't even come.

Israel

Why did the dog love us so much? Because I was stealing from my own meals and I gave it to him. Once Ludwig came to me and said like this, "Well! I brought you some beautiful piece of meat with no bones." That piece of meat was horsemeat, I smelled it, I couldn't take it in my mouth. Later he asked me if it was good, and I said, "Yes, very good" − because I gave it to the dog.

Frania

After almost freezing to death, Israel said we have to make something: if we know that Germans are coming, and the dog is barking, we'll have the last second for somewhere to hide. You know what he made? The Germans came and they could never know that we're there. He made a hole, a bunker, under the cow. There is a stable, yes? And there was the cow, and you know, a cow is standing in the stable — so you know what she's doing, she's making all the time, it's always full there of manure. He cleaned this away, Israel, and he made a hole under the cow. And on top, we should be able to go in, he made again that same kind of cover that he made for the bunker in Pinczow. The cow was doing her business on this place but we knew how to find it: exactly where the cow had the tail. So we took off the cover, and we slid down. But the smell, you could die. I don't know, if I would have to sit there two hours, I would die. It's a good thing we didn't sit more than half an hour. One time we went there, and they were standing on top of us, the Germans. They had dogs, but never a dog could smell under all this manure. You know, I don't think they really came for Jews — just to buy eggs, or something. But you don't know — if Germans come, you're afraid and you run anyway. You understand?

❦ *FRANIA* ❦

You know, at Ludwig's was like this: we ate only that bread, without butter, without nothing, because every piece of butter Zofia made, she ran to Pinczow to sell it.

They went out in the field, every day Israel was watching at the window, and I did everything in the house: the ironing, and washing. The only thing I couldn't do is cook, because if you cook, and the door is closed, and Ludwig and Zofia work in the field, the neighbours would see that the smoke comes out the chimney — so who's inside?

Anyway, I wrote to Shaindele, that maybe she'll speak to Juzia, if she could only buy something for us when she goes to the market. I was just very weak. We needed some butter, some fat. We ate dry bread, two weeks old. Milk we didn't have much either, because they had to give it away for the contribution the Germans demanded. Potatoes, we had a bit. Ludwig was raising chickens and rabbits. When the little chicks came out of the eggs, me and Israel, we were raising them, we were helping them go out of the shells. And Ludwig — I told you, he was such a man that you could write a book about him — when he killed the chickens, if I wouldn't have seen him do it, I would eat. But you know, I raised those chickens from little chicks. You know how he killed them? The chickens were all running outside in the yard. He took a piece of wood, and with such a sadism he said, "Which chicken would you like to have for Sunday?" and he took that piece of wood and just threw it into her, and killed the chicken, just like that. And we couldn't eat it. We never ate chicken there; we raised them. And the rabbit, the same thing. The way he killed that rabbit, once, I thought I'd die. We couldn't eat any meat there.

So we had to have something. We went to the fields at night, we took some carrots, beets — but this was only in the summertime. In the wintertime we had nothing, just the dry bread. And she cooked potatoes, and a white borscht, that's all. We gave them money, so she bought some flour, and she made noodles. But she made it with ham fat, and we couldn't eat this. So I had to have a little butter, with a little onion, to fry with the potatoes, or something. So that's why we said in a letter to Shaindele, maybe she'll speak to Juzia to buy us some butter, a little cheese — you know, the farmers made such a beautiful cottage cheese there, not like here.

Anyway, Shaindele spoke to Juzia, and she said yes. Imagine she was buying for us, and she threw it down for us in that little cellar, so that Ludwig shouldn't see. Her own brother. She knew he is not eating much himself, but she said that he's got the fresh air, and he is eating some meat — he's all right. So she brought cheese, and she brought us sugar, and a lot of butter. Well, that is why we are healthy, thank God, you know, we're not sick people. Because we had good food there from Juzia —

and she was buying for us eggs. Israel said, "What do we need the eggs for, how are you going to cook them?" I said, "Don't worry." He said, "The smoke will go out the chimney." I said, "Israel, don't worry." You know, when you are in trouble, you think faster. I made scrambled eggs like you never ate in your life. Well, what did I do? They didn't have any electricity — when I had to do the ironing, I took the hot coals left over from the fire and put it all into the iron, and the iron gets hot. Well, when we were alone in the house, I didn't even have the coals because in the summertime, when Zofia went to the field, she put some water there to put it out. So what did I do? I took a little bit of the charcoal that was left, put on just a drop of kerosene we used for the little lamp that we have at night, and I started to make the fire. I took that iron, I was shaking a little bit, blowing, blowing the charcoal, till it got all good red, then I took a tiny little pot and put it right on the iron — and I made scrambled eggs, with fried onions with the black bread Zofia baked, with so much butter and cheese. I'm telling you, a feast.

And Maniek was with us — he knew everything — he was eating with us whatever we had. He knew, and he didn't tell his mother. He wasn't Ludwig's child so he was very close to Israel.

He came home once — he was so bitter — he said, "I went over to my friend's place and all the kids are sitting on the father's lap. And my father he never yet took me on his knee, never."

So Israel said, "What do you care Maniek? I'm taking you. Come sit on my knee. To me, you're just like my child. You don't have to worry about it."

He taught him writing, reading, everything. Maniek felt for us, he would give away his life. I took him to eat with us because he was so thin, so pale, he was so afraid of Ludwig's shadow — he was right away in a corner — he didn't know but he felt that this is not his father. So I took him in, and I knew that I could trust him. I never saw such a smart child in my life.

I told Maniek when we would be eating. When Ludwig and

Zofia went to the field, he had to go too. But he would say he
has to go to the toilet. Zofia said, "What do you mean, you're
going to the toilet? You have the field here — that's your toilet."
We didn't even have a toilet — you went outside in a corner,
where Ludwig threw out all the things from the stable, there
you went, that's it. So Maniek always had an excuse, he wants
to go home — because he knew that we are going to eat. So he
hardly even ate with them.

"What's the matter with you, you're not eating?"

"I'm not hungry."

He knew that if he is going to fill his stomach with those
potatoes, he won't be able later to eat his scrambled eggs that I
gave him, with the butter, with so much cheese. I said once,
"Maniek, you've got to eat a little bit, because your mother will
suspect something." Well, Maniek had a ball with this.

This food Juzia brought really kept us alive, gave us strength
— they say two eggs equal a steak — and we were young too, so
it helped.

ISRAEL

Meanwhile, Ludwig started to get nasty. Very nasty. Every day
he came home with another story: that no Jew will be alive.
And he's scared, they're going to kill him if he is keeping Jews.
So I wrote a letter to Shaindele, that she should try to write me
a letter in Polish, saying I belong to the underground, to the
partisans, but nobody knows — I'm an officer in the Polish
underground, and if I need a revolver, she will send it to me.
And I should write down who is doing bad things to the Poles
and to the Jews. I wanted that letter should fall into Ludwig's
hand. I pretended I forgot it, and left it on the table when I
went to the cellar. He took the letter and read it. The next day,

when he got up, he told me that he is surprised, he didn't understand why I didn't tell him. So I said that is a secret. He got scared, and treated us better.

We never thought what's going to be later — right now, I want to be saved. I was running away exact like a fly on the table when I touch with my finger and the fly runs away and stands somewhere else — the fly doesn't think what's going to be later. Because the events came so fast, one after another, and you found yourself thinking the opposite to what you were thinking yesterday, it was impossible to think.

What can I give you to understand, what can I tell you, when the brains are blocked. I can only remember physically what I did, I kept a diary, whatever happened in the day, but Ludwig told me, if I'm going to keep writing, he will throw me out, because if something happens the Germans will grab it, and see how long I was there. I had to throw it away. I saw, absorbed with my eyes, how it happens people can become animals.

I always got in my mind, it bothered me, in Jewish law it is not allowed, when you get up in the morning, to right away go and eat. When you're taking your feet down from the bed, right away you have to prepare yourself with a little bit water, to wash your fingers, and your eyes, and you have to say a prayer right away. After that you sit down at the table, and you're eating breakfast. That stuck with me and I couldn't understand why you have to do all that — if you're hungry, why can't you eat before? Now I'm turning to Ludwig. Five o'clock in the morning, when he just opened his eyes and sat up, right away he said to his wife, and he started to push her, "Eat! I want to eat! I want to eat!" And she had to jump down right away, if not he was so mad... At that time, the thought came to me, the difference between an animal and a human being. And it came also to me to understand what the meaning was of the lion and the deer in front of the Torah. If you have to keep back your anger, you have to be so strong, like a lion. The deer is a symbol, if you have to do a good deed, you had to run like a deer. In that time I had time to think, I understood that nobody could do right away what he wants to do: "I am hungry, I want to eat right away!" So the Jewish law says that when you get up in the morning, you're like any animal, no different. But an animal runs right away to eat, and a human being has to learn how to keep himself back, not to say, "I want now, right now, and I have to get it right now." On account of that, I understood, when I saw Ludwig, if he would wash himself, make a prayer — doesn't matter, he doesn't have to make a prayer — just wash himself, and come back to the stage of being a human being, he wouldn't be like an animal. I understood that the people who made that law couldn't talk psychologically like I am talking — in that time the people were not listening, so to turn them into human beings, they had to be given laws. And I understood, when I was at Ludwig's, why the law was given, and it helps a lot to think that everything you were doing, in the law, has a meaning, why. Today people are asking me, "Do you believe in God?" I say, "Yes, I believe in God, but I'll take him to court."

But I also understood that even a fly wants to live. I can tell you in the summertime, when Ludwig and Zofia went to church, closed the door — it was made from a few boards put together, it wasn't an elegant door — and the sun shined in between the cracks, I stood there and I saw flies coming in and out, in and out, freely. You know what that means, that word, "free"? I was talking to myself: "Imagine. That fly doesn't know anything, has a right to live, can go out on the free world and can come in." And I was jealous — why can't I be a fly and also walk back and forth on the free world, and be able to see the sun like any animal. I was jealous of the chicken outside, playing around, running around and picking from the earth, freely, nobody bothered them. Only me, a human being, I couldn't go out, and breathe, free.

✂ FRANIA ↝

I told you Ludwig had two sisters, Juzia and Wichta. Juzia was the nice one and then there was Wichta, an anti-Semite, a born one. She was terrible — you looked at her, you could see how bad she was. I know you're not supposed to say a human being is ugly, but she was the ugliest thing I ever saw. I'm telling you she looked like a witch, and Juzia looked like an angel. Two sisters.

Every Tuesday and every Friday the two sisters came to the Pinczow market to buy food and then smuggle it back to Warsaw. That's the way they survived. Whenever they came, they visited Ludwig and that Wichta would look at us — and if looks could kill…

She hated us and she only wanted Ludwig to throw us out. Each time she came, she gave him a lecture about it. "Why are you keeping them?" "Why do you need the trouble? Somebody will squeal on you and you are going to be killed. You throw them out or you are going to lose your family and your life."

You know, every time she came she was getting hotter and hotter about it and we were afraid maybe she'll talk him into it. So we thought of a plan. I think it was Juzia's idea but anyway the next Thursday night when Wichta came, Israel and me hid in that little cellar.

Ludwig said, "Wichta, I listened to you. I threw them out. They went three days ago. I told them I can't do it any more. I'm sick and tired and I'm afraid."

Wichta said, "That's good! Now I'm going to go after those two sisters of Frania in Warsaw. First I'll take all the money away from them. Later I'll give them to the Gestapo. Now it's my time. Good. Good."

And we were sitting in that cellar and heard everything. Can you imagine how we felt? Who could think that was what she would do? We just thought if she thinks we're gone, she'll stop bugging Ludwig. But now? Oh, she was like a witch.

What could we do, run out and kill her? With bare hands?

While her brother is sitting there and her sister and the little boy?

"I'm going to get those two sisters," she said.

Juzia said, "You're crazy."

She said, "I'm not crazy. That's what I'm going to do."

They slept over that night and then Friday morning they went to the market. From there they would go back to Warsaw. So we didn't even have a chance to speak to Juzia. I didn't have any way to warn Shaindele and Malkale. But I knew when Juzia got back she would for sure warn them, because this was an angel, not a woman, a heart of gold.

I used to say, "How can your brother and your sister be like this, and you are so beautiful, so nice?"

Anyway, what could we do, we just had to figure that Juzia will warn my sisters and they'll have to move out right away.

But that same day, two o'clock in the afternoon, we saw Juzia is walking into Ludwig's yard to the house. Alone.

She came in, I said, "Where's Wichta?"

"We were at the market and the Germans started to grab Polish people to go work in the factories in Germany, and they grabbed Wichta. They grabbed her right at the market and put her in a truck and that's it."

I said, "You see? We have to survive the war."

The point is that the same day Wichta said what she said — she went to the market for three years, they never got her — that day they made a round-up there and they took her. They didn't have any Jews any more, they took the Poles. They needed them probably for the ammunition factories. Listen, a few months later, the same thing happened to my sisters in Warsaw. Rounded up as Poles for work in Germany.

Frania
Maniek saved our life once.

Israel
Just once?

Frania

All right, but this time was a miracle. It was one month before the war ended. We were eating and suddenly the dog started to bark.

Israel

The dog was barking like somebody was right at the door.

Frania

And we didn't even know who's there. Maniek went right away to put his ear at the door. "You better hide," he said. "Fast." And we went into that little cellar. In a split of a second we were there.

Israel

And when I closed my cellar door, they opened the front door. Then we heard German talking, we didn't know what to do. We were just frozen, both of us. And the sweat started to run, we were just wet.

Frania

We heard the voices of two German soldiers. They're talking to the Banyas, who didn't understand what they were saying in German at all. We understood right away. They were saying they're going to sleep here tonight. That's it, I thought. We survived two and a half years, and this is the end now. Then we heard Zofia took some straw and right away put it down by our little cellar door for Maniek to sleep there. Because she was afraid that if a soldier will lie there to sleep, he's going to hear us breathing. It's impossible he should not hear — that little door, it was almost open all round the edges. So she put Maniek there. And on the other side, she put some straw for the two soldiers.

Israel

It was hard for me. You see, I had a cough, from smoking.

I put my fist into my mouth to stop myself, and I told Frania, if I'll die sitting like this, because I can't breathe, just you be quiet, so you'll be alive.

Frania

They lay down to sleep it must have been eight o'clock. And Maniek started to cry, to cough, every ten minutes that boy was crying and coughing. And the Germans, they were so mad. What are they going to do? Shoot him?

Israel

Zofia was going to him, "Maniek, what's the matter? Be quiet. Go to sleep." She didn't understand what he's doing.

Frania

And we did?

Israel

In the morning the soldiers left. Maniek said, "You don't understand a thing. I did it so you could cough there, in the cellar. To save your life."

Frania

You're going to tell me this is not a miracle? This is a miracle of miracles.

       ✎ *ISRAEL* ✎

Before the ending of the war, the Germans were fighting the Russians right near our farm, the front was right near us. At that time German soldiers hardly had what to eat, so they were stealing whatever they could from the Polish farmers. In the middle of the night, maybe two o'clock in the morning, I saw six, seven Germans are coming to take away the cow. And they were hiding, sneaking. So I was thinking fast: why they're hiding? Because they thought, maybe an officer is sleeping here. The officers used to sleep over in the farmer's houses and the regular soldiers had to sleep outside. Ludwig woke up and he saw them, too. I was scared he would get mad, he had only one cow, he would yell at them, they would find us. So I didn't hesitate at all — opened the door and started to yell at the soldiers in German: *"Was ist hier los!"* Those German soldiers looked right at me, they thought that I am an officer of the German army and they ran away. Ludwig looked at me like a hero.

⟿ FRANIA ⟾

Not long after that, I think right at the end of '44, German soldiers came into the house. We were hiding in the cellar, and we heard them say they're going to make some exercises in the field. Well, exercises with soldiers, something could happen. Our roof was straw, it could catch fire. So the Banyas had to go out of the house.

And you should see Maniek, how he cried.

"What's going to happen to Israel and Frania?"

So Ludwig said, "What's going to happen? If they're going to burn, they burn, and that's all. They can't go out."

We had to be left in the house. *Qué sera, sera.* Where will we go? He didn't want to leave us, Maniek. They dragged him. They took the cow, and they took the dog. And you should see the dog howl. He did not want to go. They pulled him, but he didn't want to move, because he knew that we were being left there in the house. Well, our life was just meant to be. So, nothing happened.

At the beginning of January '45, because the front was coming so close, the Russians and Germans fighting, we had to have somewhere to hide. The thing was the whole house could be destroyed in a second. The Banyas could go to neighbours in the village, but we, where will we go? We knew that it's already the end, the end of the war is coming.

At night Ludwig and Israel dug a hole in the field behind the house, fifty yards away, and covered it up with hay. The Germans could come any day to take everybody out of the house and level the ground there. So we had to be out. If they came, we were so pale, they would see right away that we're Jews.

We went in the hole, Israel and me. There was no air there at all. Even the little lamp we brought didn't want to stay burning. And the worms. I'll never forget it. We were sitting there three days, in the beginning of January 1945. The worms there, they didn't touch Israel, they were biting me, my body was all bleeding. Alive they were eating me up. Such white worms, flat ones, they were sucking from me blood, I was covered in blood. I don't know what it was, they didn't touch Israel, but me…what do you say to that? And I had to go out, I just couldn't be there. Israel stayed. *Qué sera, sera.*

↩ ISRAEL ↪

We were liberated on the thirteenth of January, 1945. A farmer told Ludwig that the Russians are three or four miles away, near the flour mill. But they stopped their advance. So it was a question whether to go to them, and I decided to think before I run.

I said to Ludwig, "If the Russians came so far, they will come a little bit further. I'll go out when the Germans surrender, or if the Russians surround the whole city."

I was thinking: why did the Russians only go so far and then stop? It happens the front was going back and forth. I wanted to be sure. We were thinking all night what to do. In the morning I decided I'm not going nowhere. And sure enough, the Russians pulled back, probably a few hundred miles back.

Every night we went out and we put our ears to the earth to hear if bombs are falling. When I put down my ear and I heard an echo from the bombs — it could be a hundred miles away, but we heard the echo — it was just like the greatest, nicest music.

Two weeks later, the Russians advanced again and started to bombard the Germans. But we didn't see Russians yet. At night we noticed there was fire not far from us and we were thinking that all the houses could be burned. I went out with Ludwig in the field behind the house and we dug a hole. It took us two nights to dig it, and I dug it exactly like you make a grave, but big enough for two people. Very deep so we could stand up. I covered it flat with wood, and on top of that I put hay. Then I took a stick and made a hole in the hay for air. I made the hole not straight up to heaven, but a little bit on a slant so that I should be able to look out in the morning and see what's happening.

We went into the hole just before the daybreak, Frania and me. It was cold but when we heard the shooting between the Germans and Russians it made us hot enough, believe me. Frania had to go back into the house, the worms were eating her. I stayed another two, three hours and when it was light, I looked out. I saw a German soldier walking, crazy, I didn't know what's wrong with him, he was walking back and forth, like he was lost. And suddenly he ran away.

Then from far away, I heard Ludwig was yelling with his whole soul, "Israel! Israel! Come out! The Russians are here!"

During the fighting, the Russians shot probably forty German soldiers and they put them together in one pile, maybe thirty yards in front of Ludwig's house, in the field. The farmers started to come out of their houses, and I'll never forget, they just walked around and around those bodies.

"I recognize this one," one farmer would say. And he swore at the body.

All the farmers were walking slowly around the dead Germans

in a circle, talking out loud to no one in particular, counting the indignities they had suffered. Suddenly they started to grab the boots, the shirts, the uniforms. Everything they grabbed from them. In a few minutes there was nothing but naked bodies.

A high-ranking Russian officer came into Ludwig's place, he looked at Frania and me, we were pale, white like the walls. We told him that we are Polish Jews. We saw right away, from his eyes, that we were still in trouble.

More officers came in, they sat down and asked, "Who speaks Russian? And German?" I said I can understand and speak a little bit. They wanted to know where the Germans are. I knew every corner of the area and I made them a sketch of the village and where possibly the Germans were. I also showed them where there was a German tank around three miles from us on a high hill in the forest. One officer gave the orders to shoot that down and they did it. They gathered together what was left of the Germans, they brought them out of the woods, one by one, hands in the air.

The Russians came with tanks, with trucks and mostly on foot. I was shocked when I saw them. So hungry, ripped in pieces, like beggars. But they were happy and singing. I went out to the yard and looked in the soldiers' faces, maybe I'll see a Jewish face. And I saw one. So I asked him in Hebrew, "*Amchu?*" – which means "One of us?" He did not answer, he just pushed me away and went into the house. There was sitting an officer smoking a cigarette. The soldier said to the officer, "Hey, tovarisch, give me a cigarette." The officer looked at him and said, "Shut your Jewish mouth!" The soldier answered, "I'm not a Jew, I'm Gypsy. I'm not a Jew!" That was a shock to me. And Ludwig was standing there with his mouth open because he didn't know that the Russians didn't like Jews either. I used to tell Ludwig that Stalin would put him into the Golden Book for saving two Jews.

The interesting thing was, while we were hiding for all that time, I was looking for ways and means to make Ludwig be good. I told him that he is so smart, that he should be the leader of the village, that I don't believe he could kill a fly on the wall. And I talked him into being human. When he did something brutal I said, "That is not Ludwig." So I made him believe in himself, that he should do better things. He was anxious to know what will happen after the war. He knew that we have a flour mill and I told him we will try to help him have a better life.

Later the Russians made their headquarters in Ludwig's house. And they started to curse the Germans, and the Poles. And the Jews.

FRANIA <del></del>

The Russians, when they came in, one of them saw right away that I am Jewish. He picked me up in the air, "Hurrah! *Evreiskaia Devushka!*" — that means, a Jewish girl. "Hurrah! *Evreiskaia Devushka!*"

You know, when the Russian soldiers came, Israel was always close to me. The Russians were starving for a woman. If they see that I have somebody, they wouldn't dare touch me. But the minute they see that I don't have somebody... so Israel was always close. He never went away for a second. Not for a second.

We were at Ludwig's farm eight days after they came. We wanted to be sure, before we left, that the Russians wouldn't be pushed back again. The soldiers were coming like mushrooms, we didn't see from where, the fields were full of them.

And again a miracle happened that we were alive.

We were cooking big pots of potato soups for them. And hot water to wash — they were so black from dust. I was cooking all day. When night came, I was so tired, I could hardly go on top of the stove, to my place where I slept. The soldiers slept in the house, and they slept in the stable, they slept everywhere, and how big was the whole house? From that cooking so much, all the smoke from that wood, everything went to the top and I was trying to sleep there, I thought I'm going to choke. It was terrible for that eight days. I was liberated, but I worked like a horse.

Every morning, Zofia was getting up six o'clock, it was still pitch dark, and she made the fire. And all the smoke was coming right on top to me. This was going on already for four or five days, and I knew I had to clean the ashes out of that stove then it wouldn't be so much smoke. That day... it was just meant for us to be alive. That's all.

That morning, Ludwig started to wake Zofia.

"Matka," he called her. Matka means "mama."

"Matka, time to get up. You have to make the coffee for the soldiers."

So I thought to myself: oh my God, I can't take the smoke any more. It's already six days she didn't clean that stove down there. What the hell, I'm going down, I'll do it.

"Zofia, I'm going down. I'm going to make the coffee."

She said, "No, no, I'm going."

"You stay in bed, I'm going to make it today."

And I went down, and I cleaned out that piece of iron there, all the holes, cleaned the ashes, and I see something metal in there. I said to Israel, "What is this?" I saw a little box.

"Oh my God," he said. And he took it out in the field.

It was a grenade.

One soldier, a Ukrainian, went away the night before, and I knew he was the one who put the grenade in the stove. I didn't like him, he had such terrible eyes, that man. He was such an anti-Semite, I looked at him, and I said to Israel, you could see the hate in his eyes. Before he left that night, he knew we're going to make the fire in the morning. The grenade will explode and the whole house would go. Just like that. And that day I said to her, I'm going to make the fire. She never cleaned. We would have all gone with the fire. The whole house was mostly straw. Can you imagine, what an anti-Semite this was? So what do you say to this coincidence? A miracle.

⤜⤏ ISRAEL ⤎⤕

The Russians caught an officer of the German army, but they couldn't talk to him, so they brought me to be the translator. They were keeping him in another farmer's place, not far away. I walked over there with the Russian soldiers, and sat down in front of the German. The Russian officer started asking questions: Was he at the front in Stalingrad? He said no. He was lying, because they found papers on him that said he was in Stalingrad. They asked him all kind of questions. He was lying all the time. On his chest he had the Iron Cross from Hitler.

The Russian officer gave me his gun and said, "Shoot him."

I couldn't believe he asked me to do it. But he meant it.

The Russian was yelling at me, swearing, "Shoot him goddamn you! After everything they did to you! Kill him!"

I couldn't.

Well, they took him out later to the back of the house, and as I was walking away, I heard the shot.

Finally, the Russians advanced further west. Some farmers from the village came to Ludwig's, and they wanted to kill me because they thought I'm going to squeal on them that some farmers were killing Jews.

So I made a speech, where I must have spent two hours persuading them that I am not going to do anything. I talked about the meaning of life; I told them that I don't belong to squealers; I said I don't know anything anyway, you're squealing on yourselves. I said I'm glad I'm alive, that's all and I'm going to look for my family.

Part Four

I walked with Frania into Pinczow. Two and a half years since we were there. You're trying to understand what it was like for us to be back? For us it was like a fog, we couldn't see anything. We walked into the town and Poles that recognized us said, "Oh, you're still alive?" Not with warmth, you understand, they were just curious, surprised. The stomach turned. We told them, "We're still alive."

Jews came to Pinczow that we didn't know. They came and went, came and went, looking for family, everybody was looking for family, it was just speechless moments. From a population of nine thousand people, maybe ten, twelve Jews we knew from Pinczow came back. One came with the Russian army. One came from hiding. One from the woods. Everybody was wondering who was alive.

"Maybe you saw…?" Everybody was interested about his own family.

"Did you see somebody from my family?" and they went further.

"Where are you going?"

"We don't know, we just want to look, maybe some family's left over."

It was so chaotic that you couldn't think.

We couldn't go back to Frania's house because Poles were living there, so we went to the flour mill. A Russian soldier came in, he said he heard that some Jews were staying here. I looked at his face and I asked him if he's Jewish. He was. We told him that we're Jewish too, and he fell on us and kissed us and cried his head off, and he said these words, with his crying voice, that the Germans killed his bride two days before the marriage in Odessa, and he swears to God and to the whole humanity: "It is probably a thousand miles to Berlin, if I'll live and I'll come to Berlin, whatever German I'll meet, I'll kill. I'll kill as much as my strength will keep me."

The Russians were moving west, to the front, and he couldn't stay very long. We told him that our house used to be in the town square. He said, "Don't worry, come with me and we will take the house." So we went with him and he asked the Poles very politely to give us back one room. They moved down and we moved up.

We were going to the flour mill and working every day. At first we did it by ourselves for a few days. Later the Russians came in, asked our names and said that we have no right to do anything, it belongs to the city. And they put a commissar over me. I was taking in grain and giving out flour and he was standing over my head all the time.

I sold a few hundred pounds of flour and I bought a wagon and horse for Ludwig. And he never went away without two big sacks of flour. Later on, all the farmers came: "Why didn't you come to me to hide, why didn't you come to me?" After everything, they were all smart.

Frania

You know, at that time we used to go from Pinczow to visit the Banyas. The minute we got to the little hill — it was still half a mile to the house — that dog smelled us already and he came running to us.

Israel

He was so excited, he didn't know what to do.

Frania

He came running! And Maniek, when he saw that we were free, he was very happy.

Israel

I still have it in the back of my mind, if I could afford it, I would bring him here for a visit.

Frania

He has a wife and four children. I don't think that he could come. The government wouldn't let him out.

Israel

They would let him come for a visit if they knew that his wife and children were still there. And that's what I would like to see once more in my life. Maniek.

Frania

Yes, but I'm going to tell you something. If we wanted to do it, it's not so much money, we could bring him here. But the point is, he would never understand how we live. If he would come, he would think really that I am a millionaire. So why bring him? Just to satisfy myself? To go there to see him there, and Zofia, to bring them some money, that will be enough satisfaction for me.

Israel

To go back is not such an easy thing.

Frania

I wouldn't go to Pinczow at all. There's no Jews. Nobody. And the memories… I would just go straight to Zofia and Maniek. And then leave.

Israel

Anyway, we used to go visit them at that time, and when we left, I saw with my eyes that the dog knew and went crazy. I actually saw the dog with tears in his eyes when he felt that we were going away.

Frania

Later, we found out what happened to my uncle Itchele from Dzialoszyce — the one who gave me the money to open the store, before my marriage. He went with his son Leibick to a farmer he knew so well — he used to buy grain from him — and that farmer hid them. Six months before the war finished, the farmer killed them. Imagine.

Israel

There was no big shortage of cruelty. How about her uncle Meyer, what he did to us?

Frania

What do I have to talk about that? Why mix in such terrible things?

Israel

Well, that is a real story.

Frania

So, it's a real story. So what? A lot of families, you see that they're selfish.

Israel

No, this is a story that is cruel.

Frania

So it's cruel, so what can you do?

Israel

Her family…

Frania

You know what, listen, I am going to tell you something: you keep your family on that side and I'll keep mine on this.

Israel

All right.

Frania

This uncle Meyer – he was a brother to my mother. Before the war he married a girl from Miechow. They had a little boy, two years old. And his wife, oh! she was a beautiful girl. The first round-up the Germans took was the Jews from Miechow. Meyer paid so much money to find out where they took his wife and child. Nobody could find out. Meyer survived. He was hidden at a farmer's.

Israel

He was hidden not far from Pinczow, at the house of the leader of the anti-Semites, in his place he was hidden. That man was the head of the Polish Nationalists Partisans, the A.K. — Armia Krajowa. They fought the Germans, but if they found Jews hidden somewhere, that man gave the orders to kill them all. But he was hiding Meyer. Meyer was so rich, he promised him, if he will survive, he will give him everything and sign it to him.

Frania
He gave him plenty, don't worry.

Israel
So he hid him in a drawer. You opened the door to a big wardrobe, and there were drawers, big ones. Meyer was a tall man…

Frania
He must have been six feet.

Israel
But he lived in a drawer. He couldn't read, couldn't do nothing, just eat, and sleep. It took him a half a year to shave. He picked with his hand every hair from his face.

Frania
You know, he had such a habit later that I always slapped him, slapped him because he always was picking hairs off his face.

Israel
He couldn't walk.

Frania
He couldn't straighten his legs, after laying like that so long — three years.

Israel
In that time, we were already a few days free. A Pole came in and said, "Your uncle is alive."

Frania
We didn't know that he's alive, and when we went out we saw him coming down the hill, crawling, he couldn't

walk. Well, I don't have to tell you, we took him in, and I washed him, and what I didn't do for this man, you just can't imagine.

Israel
We worked on him — months.

Frania
But he couldn't swallow it, that I am alive with my husband. Listen, he was young too, you know, and jealousy was just eating him up alive. He knew that I did everything for him, to put him back on his feet. I'm telling you, what I didn't do, what I didn't cook for him. And I really cared, after all, how many uncles did I have left? And I didn't know yet about my sisters, I didn't know that I have anybody left over. Meyer was jealous that Israel is alive. He figured if Israel was dead, Meyer could marry me. But if I have Israel, so what does Meyer have? Nobody. Nothing.

Israel
After we were at the flour mill a few weeks, Shaindele and Malkale came back alive. They were working in a factory in Germany, and there Shaindele met Jean, a Frenchman, a Catholic. They fell in love. So he was with them when they came back to Pinczow.

Frania
Naturally they came to Pinczow. Where else would they go? They wanted to see if someone's alive. Well we fell on each other and cried. Meyer was saying always, "I don't need anything, I don't live for myself. I only live for the children." Only for the children — that meant us. You know talk is cheap. He only wanted to marry Malkale. He saw Shaindele he cannot have — and, by the way he wanted to talk her out of Jean, but she told him to go to hell — I had Israel, so he wanted Malkale, and he went

after her. He said, "If you're not going to marry me, I'm going to take my life." She said, "I'm sorry, I can't help it. I like you as an uncle, but I'm not going to marry you, forget it." She was only eighteen years old. So I guess from bitterness, who knows from what, anyway, he didn't give us anything. Later, he sold the flour mill, the houses, and whatever he sold, you know how much money he had?

Israel

I said to my dear wife, "Your uncle wouldn't give you a cent, he's so egotistical. I'm working my head off at the mill for nothing because if I give the money to him, I tell you he won't give us a cent. Frania, I'll give you our money, and hide it."

Frania

I said, "Hide the money? My uncle is going to cheat *me?*" "You heard," he said. "He lives only for us, what do you mean he's going to cheat me. I'm not going to hide the money."

Israel

He wasn't like that before the war.

Frania

Maybe he was and we didn't know it.

Israel

I have to tell you about what I am now certain. A human being is basically an animal. The environment keeps him back to be normal — just the environment. Sometimes the society, sometimes parents, family. When they lose their family, they have no shame, the whole badness from the animal comes out free, because he's not scared, nobody will tell him off. And that was a hundred percent that uncle Meyer. We took him in, took care of him and he could still say, "You are alive!? You are alive!? You shouldn't be. My wife should be alive, not you." Just plain

said that to me. I was crying my head off, and I told
Frania, "He's cruel." After everything, after helping him,
after carrying him on my hands, from bed to the toilet.

   Meyer came to the girls, to Shaindele and Malkale, and
Frania and he said, "Children, I live only for you. But you
wouldn't be able to sell all those houses that belong to
you, to all of us. Give me a blank signature, and I'll be able
to sell."

Frania

Oh, we were then fools.

Israel

They gave him the blank signature. He sold everything.
Not less than a quarter of a million dollars.

Frania

He didn't give us a cent.

Israel

Wait. He sold everything, and bought gold. The gold he
hid in a bread, a round bread, twenty inches in diameter.

Frania

The bread was long.

Israel

Oh no, I'll never forget it, a round bread. He took it with
him to Lodz. He was so cruel — I'd spit him right now in
the face, if I could. He's still alive.

   He took all the money. And the truth is he wrote a letter
recently to Moishe Finkelstein, my cousin, if it's possible
to take him over here to Canada. And I told Moishe to
write him, if he needs bread, I'll send him a bread and put
poison in it.

Frania

Ah, what's revenge?

Israel

My cousin Moishe Finkelstein arrived in Pinczow. He was

looking for family too, he didn't know who was alive or not. Whenever Jews came into the town, the Poles told them that a Jewish family is alive and stays in the flour mill. Everybody who came, came to us. Moishe was living in Lodz and before he was taken to concentration camp, he knew what happened to my family in the ghetto. I was afraid to ask.

Frania
Right away Moishe told him, "Everybody's dead."

Israel
He told me that my older brother, Chaim-David, went to the wires that surrounded the ghetto and got electrocuted. On purpose. He couldn't bear it any more. And the rest of the kids died from starvation. Moishe told me my father buried them all.

I asked about my father. Moishe said the Germans wanted him to squeal on somebody about some possessions they were hiding. He did not want to squeal so they broke him — the hands and the legs — piece by piece — he should talk. He did not tell them. They physically destroyed him and he did not say a word.

Frania
First the father buried all the kids and then Moishe buried the father.

Israel
Anybody who is alive feels guilt. "Why not me? Why them?" Maybe if I would be there, maybe I could help.

Frania
This cannot help, this thinking.

Israel
Because I was the most capable. No one else could go without an armband, and when I was there, I used to bring bread.

Frania

But Israel, why should you think like this? It was meant to be that way.

Israel

It could be, if I would be with them, maybe it would be different.

Frania

Yes, but you were young. And you were in love and wanted to come to me, so what's the use of talking? If I wouldn't be pregnant, I wouldn't be sitting here. I would have gone to Lublin, then to Majdanek and I would be the first one in the ovens. So you see? Luck, it's only luck. Who survived, it's only by luck. It's not that you were smarter or something like that. It was just meant to be. Anyway, we were in Pinczow with Shaindele and Malkale and the stories started. Those stories, they go on till today. I knew already that my parents and my brother Chamel were dead in Majdanek. We heard this already from the letters we got from Shaindele while we were still hiding.

Israel

Her brother Chamel was grabbed to Majdanek when he was in Lublin. Majdanek is just on the outskirts of the city. Somebody squealed on him and the Gestapo caught him.

Frania

Half an hour before they caught him, he gave all the money he saved, in gold, to Shaindele. She was looking out the window and saw how they grabbed him. She knew he was betrayed by somebody so she took Malkale and they ran fast to Warsaw.

Israel

We made up that whatever will happen, anything, we

should write to a Polish woman in Lublin that Chamel knew.

Frania

She was a very nice person. And her place was like a depot, from her we'll have all the information about the others who survived, or who is where. Anyway, I don't know how he did it but Chamel smuggled out of Majdanek a letter to Lublin, to this Polish woman. A letter for Shaindele. "So much money I gave you, can't you even send me a loaf of bread? I'm starving. Don't I deserve you should help me?" So when Shaindele received this letter, she couldn't stop sobbing. But she went. Right into Majdanek. As a Pole. She walked in together with other Polish workers. There was a little building there, like an office. She went in there, there was a man working, believe it or not, she recognized this man right away. He used to live in the same apartment building as my grandfather in Lublin. He was a rabbi's son. David was his name. Young — maybe twenty-five. He didn't recognize her but she knew who he was right away. She said, "Listen, I am looking for Chamel Greenfeld, I was sent here by his sister, Shaindele, they paid me very well. I want you should help me out somehow to smuggle in bread for Chamel, because Shaindele told me that he is starving." She talked in Polish, like she would be a *shiksa*. She didn't know what was what, she didn't want to trust him just like that.

He said, "I know Chamel very well. We'll see what we can do." Suddenly, he saw outside the Germans are running, it's a whole commotion. He said, "Oh my God, what's going on?" And he opened a door, there was little room with a bed. He said, "Go in there, if they see you here, I'm right away in trouble." He pushed her in there, they shouldn't see her. Luckily when the Germans came

in, they didn't open that door. If they had, then she would
be finished. They shot a lot of Poles they thought maybe
were Jewish, or helping Jews. It was already five o'clock
and it started to get dark, and he said, "Listen. You cannot
go out now because it's going to look suspicious. It's not
good for me, it's not good for you because the Germans
are still running around out there and I'm afraid. You have
to stay overnight and then in the morning you go out.
Working people are coming in so then you could mix, but
at night nobody's going anywhere." So what could she do?
He told her, "You lie on the bed and I'll sit on the chair."

Anyway, listen, he was a young man — he didn't have a
woman, for who knows how long — and he must have
thought to himself: she's a Gentile girl — who cares? And
he was really getting hot, hot. He was ready for anything.
She saw what's going to happen. She was a virgin. So then
she started to cry. Then she talked in Yiddish: "Listen,
David," she called him by name. "I am not a Polish girl. I
am Chamel's sister Shaindele. And please, I told a lie
because I was afraid." It was just like somebody would
pour on him a bucket of cold water. He was just so pale
like chalk, all his blood left him, like she got his throat.
She'll never forget, she said, that scene. Naturally. And he
didn't touch her. She walked out of the camp in the
morning. And he promised that he'll buy the bread for
Chamel. He didn't even want to take money from her. But
the main thing, she said, "Tell him I was here." But later
she never heard any more from our brother Chamel.

My father was also in Majdanek. Three letters I have
from him, that he smuggled out, he must have found a
man in the camp to deliver the letters to this Polish
woman in Lublin. Shaindele gave me these letters after
the war. I have them here. You see, they are written in
pencil on the back of a paper bag. In Polish "Dear lady, I

wrote a few time to my daughters to send me some money but I didn't receive an answer. I'm sending this letter with a man — please give him a hundred zlotys for me. And write to my children to leave some money for you, so that you could send some to me. So far I am well, but I don't have any strength because I have nothing to eat. Where is my son Chamel?" — you see he didn't know Chamel was in Majdanek too — "… and where are my daughters? About my wife, I don't know anything." This is dated the twelfth of December 1942.

"Dear lady. I received the hundred zlotys for which I thank you very much. I could buy for this money a piece of bread. I continue to live. Please send with this man two hundred fifty zlotys. This will last me a little while. I'll write you again, if I'll be alive. And please write me about my children. I thank you for everything." He signed it: S.B. Greenfeld. 13th Dec. 1942.

"Dear lady. Save me from dying from starvation. Please give three hundred zlotys to this man for me because it's very hard to get hold of this man if I need him, and it's also very costly, I have to pay him for it, for taking this letter. My Dear Lady, if you could somehow let my son Chamel know, he'll send you for sure the money back. But in the meantime if you send me the money, not to wait any time, so you'll save my life from hunger. And this could only last just for a short little, little time. I would be able to buy with this only dry bread. And please, my Dear Lady, write me how much you're sending." (I suppose he wanted to know how much this man took out before he gave it to him)…"if it takes time for you to get in touch with Chamel, maybe you could sell some of the things I left with you. But I beg you, send me money in the meantime. Save my life for which I thank you very much." And this one is signed: S.B. Greenfeld 15/12/42.

❧ ISRAEL ❧

We stayed in Pinczow till May of '45 and then we had to run to
Lodz. The Polish anti-Semites — the partisans — came to the
flour mill to kill us. It was lucky, when the Germans were
operating the mill during the war, they were scared of the
partisans too, so they made iron doors. When the partisans
came, they couldn't get in. A day later we took a bus to Kielce.
We heard that the Poles made a pogrom and there killed over a
hundred Jews a year later in 1946. It wasn't safe for us in small
towns. We took the train to Lodz, but on the way we had to
pretend to be Poles because the Poles were still killing the Jews.
And the Russians didn't even mix in.

From all the little towns, from all over the area, whoever
survived, came back. It took a few months, they came. From
towns with populations of thousands came back two, three.
And then they couldn't stay in their own towns — no parents,
nobody. So where did they go? To a point where more Jews are.
Everybody was running to Lodz. Warsaw mostly was burned.

So we came to Lodz and we stayed with my cousin Moishe. I
didn't have any money so I started to look for work. And Frania
and I wanted to have our own place. I found a job working in a
factory with knitting machines, like before the war. And an
apartment I found too. It belonged to a Gestapo. He probably
took it during the war from a Jewish family, and now it was
deserted. We moved in. Just like that. It was wide open. When
we went into the house, it was everything intact. Even a fork
and a knife, pots and pans, everything.

I used papers that identified me as a Pole, Josef Lewitski.
Why? I'll give you an example. Before the war there was on that
street alone probably ten thousand Jews. After the war was five
Jewish people. From ten thousand, five. When we were sitting
there in our apartment, came in a neighbour. He was a
Communist — he didn't know I'm a Jew — and he said to me,

"Comrade Lewitski, the whole street is again with Jews."

So I said, "How many?"

"I don't know, I see them everywhere."

Altogether was maybe five Jews. That was the personality of my neighbour the Communist. He said, "It's something wrong, your wife looks Jewish." So I said to him, "She is a convert."

That was in 1945 when the Russians were already there. After two weeks the radio said that two Jews were living on another street, it was just an announcement. And they were killed. After liberation. After coming back from concentration camps.

I went out on the street and at that time, in 1945, walking in the street, you could see people with pale faces, the hair cut off from the camps — you could recognize right away who is Jewish and who not. Later on, I found a Jewish community centre. Really, it was just an office and whoever came in wrote his name down, in case somebody wanted to know if you're alive. Everybody who came in was looking for family. That was the only place you could go in that time. And everybody wanted to know, how did you survive, how did *you* survive? Hundreds and hundreds of people used to come every day. Looking at lists. At faces.

Frania

We wrote a letter to Ludwig and he came to visit us in Lodz. That was the summer of 1945. I went out with him to the market to buy a chicken. I'll never forget. You know, they were selling there live chickens? I'm telling you, it was so funny, he was so proud of himself, the way he took that chicken to see if it was fat enough, like a professional. I bought the chicken, I made dinners for him and we treated him like a king. He enjoyed it.

Israel

We gave Ludwig more love than he understood even. He was proud of himself that he saved us.

Frania

He stayed a week. Later when he went home, I had to buy two valises for all the things we gave him. He could hardly carry everything.

Israel

After he left something amazing happened with Shaindele and Malkale on the street. You see, they were living in Lodz with us.

Frania

Let me tell it. First, you know that during the war, Malkale and Shaindele lived in Warsaw on false papers as Poles. Where they were living they had some neighbours too. One day they got up, and looked out the window and they were not far from the Jewish ghetto. That was when the Germans were bombing the ghetto after the resistance, and they could see from their window that the ghetto was burning. For days it was burning. You can imagine their hearts. Suddenly came in a man, a neighbour, and he said to them: "Hey girls! Look how the Jews are frying there! Like chickens!" And laughed his head off. And they had to laugh too. If not — the Poles were such anti-Semites — if you wouldn't laugh, they would accuse you that you are Jewish. So my sisters had to celebrate the burning of the ghetto. They could not forget that incident. Well, the war ended, we were all walking in the street in Lodz after the war, suddenly the girls, Malkale and Shaindele, stopped, they couldn't believe their eyes: they saw the man that came in to them when the ghetto was burning. And, he saw them. They both stopped. And he ran over and yelled at them: "You remember that time when the ghetto was burning? I looked all over for you to take revenge on you because you are Poles and I wanted to find you to show you I cheated the Germans, I cheated the Poles, I cheated everybody, and you too! I am a Jew!" So Shaindele heard this, she didn't say anything for a second. "Is that so? That's beautiful. Good luck to you. And you know what? You better sit down, I've got something to tell you. We are Jewish too."

Israel
So he stood in the street, with open mouth and he couldn't talk. He was looking for revenge! And he nearly fainted. On the pavement, on the street, he sat down.

Frania
It was such a shock to him.

Israel
He couldn't move. Because he wanted to take advantage, so he cheated the Germans, and he cheated the Poles. And he cheated himself too. It's a joke, but it's not so funny.

Frania
And then we were talking, we went out for coffee.

Israel
It always comes to crying, you know.

Frania
Sure.

Israel
And what is crying? Crying was a defence from talking and crying was an expression that I'm speechless.

Frania
You can laugh from joy and cry from joy, don't you see that?

Israel
But that is a classic. Just classic. "Look how the Jews are frying," he said. There must have been tears in his heart at that time, but he was scared.

Frania
Listen, all three of them were scared in that room.

Israel
After that Shaindele and Jean went away to Paris, on false papers. They wanted to get married. Malkale stayed with us.

Frania
Israel's cousin Moishe had staying with him two Russian officers, both of them Jewish. One was a young man, the other one was Major Zorin, he was in his sixties — what a nice man he was. The young one was such a handsome man, and he was crazy about Malkale. The older one, Major Zorin, said to me, "Look, he's my friend, but you have to see that your sister does not go with him. He cannot remain here. What will he do, desert the Russian army? Is she going to go to Russia with him?" He closed the windows, he closed the doors, he whispered to us, "Children, run away because it's coming very bad times here. Run! And fast! You lived through such a war. Run, I don't care where, just run out of Poland."

Israel
I started to ask questions at the Jewish community centre. I met some people that I knew before the war, and they told me that there is a possibility that I can get out of Poland. I should go to Zawadska Street number sixteen. They'll make the arrangements for me. It's a story that I'll never forget. I came there, I knocked on the door. "Come in." I opened the door and it was altogether dark, you couldn't see a thing. Suddenly a light came up, like a spotlight right on my face, so bright I couldn't see who was behind the light. "Israel, we know you. We know who you are." They knew everything about me, what school I went to, my father's name, everything. And they tested me, to prove I am me. "We cannot tell you who we are."

They told me that because the Communists are in Lodz, it is secret, they cannot reveal their names. They said they have sixty Jews that want to go out of Poland. I said, "Where are they?" They said, "That we will tell you later. But you will be the leader. You'll get a sign, a code number. You must go to Krakow. At the train station will come to you a man, he will tell you the code number, and he will show you the sixty people. You must tell these people not to speak to anyone. If someone asks them questions, they should send him to you. That's all that I have to tell you. On a certain day I'll tell you when you're going to go to Krakow." I didn't know anything, who they are, what they are. A few days went by, they sent a man to me, he told me I should be prepared to go to Krakow, right away.

Frania
At that time my uncle Chaim came back alive from Russia. My father had three brothers: Meyer — you know what kind of character he had; Leon — this was the uncle who wanted to marry me before the war. He survived. In fact he already had a factory in Lublin, right away. And the last brother, the best one, was Chaim. Chaim ran to Russia when the war broke out. Now he didn't want to stay with his brother Meyer or Leon, just with us. Well, when Israel told me we had to go right away to Krakow, we went with Chaim and also with Malkale. But we left in such a hurry that the few pieces of jewellery that I had left from my mother, I forgot them on the bed.

Israel
We came to the Krakow station, a man came up to me and told me the code number. He showed me the sixty people, they were there at the station — children, elderly people, young people, all kinds of people. From all over, from Hungary, Lithuania, and from Poland, all Jews, all refugees. The man said that me and Frania's uncle Chaim

and another man, Chaskel Rosenblatt, would be the
trustees, the leaders. We have to go with everybody to
another town, Katowice. It wasn't far. He gave me an
address, and he told me I should knock three times on
the door and a man will open with a very big moustache.
I should tell that man I have sixty sacks of flour, and he
will ask me how much is a sack, and I should say a
hundred zlotys a sack. We went. Nobody recognized that
there's something special about us, or that we were even a
group. In Katowice it happened just like the man said.
The new contact gave me sixty Greek passports. And he
taught me also a few Greek words: "*kalinikta, kalispera,*"
good-night and good-afternoon, or something like that.
Also he told me to go out and buy for everyone berets,
and I went out in Katowice and bought sixty berets. He
told us to go to Bratislava in Czechoslovakia and he gave
us an address.

At the border, the Polish border, the Poles stopped us
and took us out from the train and didn't let us go further.
I told our people to remember not to speak to each other,
nothing. If somebody speaks to them in Polish, just
answer them with some Hebrew prayers, for example,
say Kaddish to them, and the Poles will think it's Greek.
The Polish border officials stopped us, they talked to us
in Polish and nobody understood. We were supposed to
be coming from concentration camps, we had to be able
to talk at least a few words in German. We said only
"*Nichts verstehen.*" "We don't understand." But the Poles
also spoke a few words of German. "Passports." And we
gave them passports. So they took the passports, and the
passports said we were Greek. We had hidden money – a
little bit, not much – in soup cans, and we put in stones so
that it would have the right weight. All of us had our
money hidden this way because we knew that the Poles

would search us. The Poles made us put out everything
on the table: we had bread, we had salami...

Frania
They took away from us the salami and a few cans. The
real soup cans, but not the ones with the money. Just
lucky. I had with me a carpet, a small one, but beautiful.
They said that is smuggling and took it away.

Israel
I don't know what the Poles did with other people, but
they put us in jail for the night. That night the guards
were walking, sneaking around to see if we're Polish Jews.
Maybe we'll talk between ourselves Yiddish, or Polish.
They couldn't find out. A funny thing was that Frania was
wearing high boots and the Poles right away recognized
that these were boots from Greece, but the boots were
made in Poland. And they started to talk between
themselves: "They are Greek people, we have to let them
go, we don't want to start up with Greece." Of course we
understood every single word. They didn't let Polish Jews
out of Poland. Why, I don't know. In fact, I don't think
they let any Poles out. People were smuggling out anyway,
by foot and by bicycle and by train. Not only Jews, Poles
left too, anti-Communists ran out because they were
scared of what the Russians will do to Poland. But we
were "Greeks" so the next day they let us go.

We went on the train to Czechoslovakia, we came to
the station in Bratislava, and they stopped us: "Where are
you going?" So everybody pointed at me and the station
master came to me and I told him, in German, that we are
Greeks who were in the camps in Poland and now we
want to go home. The station master said to me very
politely, that since we are going to Greece, he has a Greek
refugee here at the station and he should go with us. Can

you imagine the kind of situation I was in? He brought over that Greek man, and he embraced me and kissed me and started to talk Greek to me. And what did I do? I answered him in Hebrew. He looked at me like I'm a crazy person. So I had to make up my mind right away: I could not take him with me. I told the station master in German: "This man is not a Greek. I just spoke Greek to him and he doesn't understand a word." And the Greek man didn't understand the German I was speaking to the station master. They took him away — where and what, I don't know. It bothered me very much, but what could I do? He was one man and we were sixty.

We went further. In Bratislava already we saw a lot of Jews from all over Europe, from Russia, Hungary, Roumania, Germany, Poland. I have to mention that the Czechoslovakian people were so kind and so nice to us, I have no words to thank them. You know how they were taking revenge on the Germans? During the war the Czechs were not allowed to walk on the sidewalk, where the Germans were walking. Only on the street. So now they reversed it. The Germans were walking only on the street. Anyway, I went with Chaim and Chaskel to the address that we had and I found out the organization helping us was the "Bricha," specially sent from Israel to help the Jews from the Holocaust get out from Communist hands. We stayed at the community centre just a few days. One night a man from the Bricha came and he said that tonight, now, we are going to cross the border. We went to a bridge that crosses from Czechoslovakia to Austria. On that bridge were standing Russian soldiers. The Bricha man went to them, bribed them with vodka, and he drank with them. "Cross," he said to us. We walked the bridge and the Russians soldiers made like they don't even see us. And we went through to Austria.

In the middle of the night we got on a train and arrived

in Vienna. The Bricha led us to the Rothschild Hospital. To that big hospital came all the Jews that ran away from the Communist countries, from all over Eastern Europe. There were hundreds and hundreds of people. A family got one bed, not more. There were children, grown-ups, old people, all categories of characters, doctors, lawyers, intellectuals, all kinds of people. They gave us a little bit to eat, but the worst part of it was that we didn't have any hot water. I took two spoons and I put a piece of wood in the middle, connected two wires to the spoons and connected it to the electricity and put it into a glass of water. After a few seconds, the water was boiling. I was the talk of the town, in that Rothschild Hospital. Everybody came to me for a little bit of warm water. They told me that I made a miracle. We were there quite a few days.

Later, there were some dignitaries from England, some committee for refugees and they started to ask everybody, "Where do you want to go?" All of us said we wanted to go to Israel. They started to laugh, they asked, "How can you go? Palestine is forbidden to take refugees. You are in Vienna, how can you go to Palestine? By train? By water?" All of us, we laughed. "It was forbidden to walk the streets in Poland. We walked. It was forbidden to stay alive. We lived. It was forbidden to leave Poland. We are here. Don't you worry, by hook or by crook, we will be in Israel." By this time we knew we had to get to Munich which was the biggest centre for refugees in that part of Europe. From there, who knows?

The Bricha later changed our Greek passports for Austrian ones. These new papers said that we are Jews from Innsbruck. On the train to Munich were two American officers and they started to talk to us in English, and we couldn't understand a word. But we had in our group a girl from Lithuania, highly intelligent, she spoke Polish, Russian, Lithuanian, German, English, and French. The officer asked her from where we are coming and where we are going. Well, she told him that we are Innsbruck Jews, returning home. They wrote down everything, the Americans. That worried us. Sometime later they got off the train, a jeep was waiting for them. On the way to Munich, the train stopped in Innsbruck. At the station was waiting for us those two officers with the mayor of the city and a whole orchestra to greet the Jews back to their "hometown," Innsbruck. Can you imagine how we felt? And the mayor gave a speech. And *none* of we were from Innsbruck. We had to stay. At least for a few days. The train left without us. We thanked everybody and asked where is the Jewish community centre. We came in there, I went in to the president and told him who we are really, and he said for us to wait here and he'll help us. We waited, we stayed there a few days. That's when the group of sixty split up. Some went to Italy and from there to Israel. Some went other places.

I heard there was a place for refugees nearby, in Genadenwald, in the hills. A resort. During the war it was used as a health spa for high Nazi officers, for skiing, beautiful dry air. I heard that there's place for over a hundred and twenty people and only fifty were staying there. We wanted to have a little bit rest, we were tired from wandering. I went to that president of the community centre and I spoke to him very politely. I said there's only fifteen of us left in our group and we would like to go to Genadenwald. "Impossible," he said. "There's no room." I went out, and talked to Chaim and to Chaskel. "We are going back in there and I'm going to do something about it, but don't laugh. No matter what I say." I went in, Chaskel on one side of me and Chaim on the other. I told the president: "I am not any more the same man that I was an hour before. I have a knife with me. The Germans killed my parents. They killed my brothers, my sisters.

I'm not scared of anything. Now I want to have a place where to sleep and to eat. And if you're not going to give it to us, I'll put my knife right into you. I am giving you five minutes time to get a bus here to take us to Genadenwald. If not, you will be with a head shorter. Not more than five minutes!" And then I looked at my watch. He turned white. Right away he called for a bus and it took us to Genadenwald. When we came there, I was walking like a leader, I ordered: I want this, and I want that. We really had a hell of a time. Everybody was scared of me, and I couldn't even kill a fly on the wall.

Frania

I'll never forget, we met there a man — I don't remember now his name — but I can picture him. Young, maybe twenty-eight. This man got so warmed up to Israel and me. It's funny, you know, that the whole life we went through, me and Israel, we had so much luck with people. People liked us so much! The minute we met somebody, they didn't let go. Maybe we had a sense of humour. We had friends, all our life. This man in Genadenwald, I'll never forget him, he said, "You two are married?" I said, "Yes." "I hope you'll have children." I said, "I hope so. But my husband doesn't want to think about it. We lost a child in the war." He said, "I was in a camp and a doctor there used me as his experiment. I can never have any children." And he started to cry so much, that I'll never, never forget it. We stayed in that beautiful resort for a couple of weeks. It was like a dream. The weather was gorgeous and we met such nice people.

Israel

After two weeks we got already tired sitting. We left and went to Munich. It was a city full of refugees from all over. We were thinking only to get out of Europe.

Frania
To go to Israel.

Israel
We weren't thinking about America at all.

Frania
We came into Munich, we went first to the community centre, they gave us an address and they said, "Germans are living at this house but here is a paper which will allow you to move in." We went, Israel, me, Malkale, my uncle Chaim, and Chaskel Rosenblatt. A German was living there with his wife and a daughter.

Israel
We found out later that man was a Nazi.

Frania
Not just a Nazi. An SS officer.

Israel
He treated us royally. He fell down so low, that big Nazi, that he took our shoes…

Frania
Every night we put our shoes by the door and he took them and shined them.

Israel
Every other minute he asked us if we need something.

Frania
He was scared of us. He knew we were survivors.

Israel
In 1945 all the Germans were scared. In his library we found albums with pictures of him in his Nazi uniform. He told us, "I had to do everything the *Führer* said. We all had to do it. But I didn't know about any killings. I don't know about any concentration camps."

Frania

Nobody knew anything. Sure it was a big secret that was kept by millions of people.

Israel

We were there with these German people only a few days, because we wanted to be together with other Jews. We went back to the centre in Munich and they gave us papers to go to the displaced persons camp called Föhrenwald. You remember?

Frania

November 5th, 1945. You know what Föhrenwald was? The Germans used to have an ammunition factory there. Now it was a refugee camp with maybe 1500 families.

Israel

We knocked in the middle of the night on the door of the leader of the Föhrenwald camp. He answered the door and we were told that there's no place for anybody. I got mad. "We are here, and we're going to stay here," I said. In the middle of the camp was a big lecture hall, like an empty theatre. We went in there, and I went out again to that leader of the camp. "I want mattresses for all our people. If not, you're not going to sleep tonight." I learned already that with politeness, I'm not going to get anywhere. I told him off and said if he's not going to do it, I'll take all the twelve people that were with me, and we will go into his house, and he wouldn't be able to do nothing about it. He brought mattresses. There were kids with us and they needed something to eat. I made him bring milk for the kids. We were there all night. In the morning, we went to the camp office for a place to live. They gave us an address in the camp to go.

Frania

All the streets in the camp were named after America. Pennsylvania Street, Missouri Avenue, Tennessee.

Israel

Every block of houses had a boss, the block leader. We were sent to Illinois Street where the block leader was a Hungarian man. He told us that in his block there was no place. We went to look, we saw there's some places there and we figured out that he probably was saving it for a whole bunch of his friends, but they didn't come yet. He said, "No, I'm keeping space for my family." I said, "We are here, your family is still in Hungary." I told him that we had from the office an order to live there. He said he doesn't believe it. I said, "If you don't believe it, go to the office and ask them." A lie? Sure it was a lie. He said, "I'm going to ask." He went and in the meantime we moved into the houses. We went back to that empty theatre, took some chairs, mattresses, and moved in. When he came back, I said to him, "Mister, as you can see, we live here now. When your family will come from Hungary, in that time we will think again."

Frania

He couldn't do anything about it. We were in already. Nine of us were living there.

Israel

After a few weeks, the office put a Hungarian couple in with us. You remember?

Frania

They were fighting like cat and mouse. She threw him out, he always slept in the hallway. We were in one big room, everybody had their separate corner.

Israel

The camp was like a small city, with all the facilities. There were already around five thousand survivors there.

As the survivors from all over Europe left their birth-
places, they came to the transit camps. There were lots of
these camps in Germany. Most of us were hoping to go to
Israel as fast as possible. But in the meantime people
started slowly to live a little bit of a normal life. Everybody started to do something positive. The so-called
government of Föhrenwald had a mayor, aldermen, its
own police force, a jail; there was a cultural office, and all
kinds of schools, from kindergarten to professional training.
It was only a transit camp but they tried make it in such a
way that everything should be just right. The whole thing
was operated by the United Nations Relief and Rehabili-
tation Administration – UNRRA.

Frania
You know how many children were born there in that
time? I heard later that these camps had the highest
birth-rate in Europe after the war. Every day we went to a
central kitchen for our provisions. We didn't like to go
stand in line there, and besides, the kitchen was terrible,
so we bought things, and I cooked myself. We had a little
oven, and I used to make big pots of soup for everybody.
Later on we travelled to Munich quite a few times. To an
opera, to the theatre. Movies. Near us was the town of
Wolfratshausen. It was only two miles, you could walk it.
Oh, the stores, it was wonderful. I found there a dress-
maker, I chose materials and a German lady was making
me clothes when the camp gave me dresses that didn't fit.
We still had a little money but you could get things
practically for nothing. But the best was coffee. If you had
some coffee, for coffee they gave you everything, the
Germans.

Israel
The first few months we were just walking around and
looking, looking, maybe we will find somebody from our

family. Every day survivors came from all over Europe. People started to look for some entertainment. The schools created some children's theatre. They had also choirs, they made concerts. We had a lot of good musicians. There was a teacher who started a theatre there and he did it with some enthusiasm. He encouraged those who were professionals before the war. People played, amateurs too. I remember an older man named Wisokodworski came forward, he said that he was a professional actor in Lithuania before the war, and he took over that theatre that the schoolteacher created. I didn't associate with him and his group, and when I saw his first play I saw I was right, because I didn't like his directing methods. In the meantime, there was created a special culture committee to look after theatres and concerts. At the same time a man called Jacob Sandler set up another acting troupe called Mapalim. He put on very nice, good plays. The people liked them very much. Jacob Sandler lives in Toronto today. By the way, we had a weekly newspaper called *Bamidbar*, which means "in the desert," and they wrote very good reviews. I saw all the plays in Föhrenwald, all the concerts. That empty theatre they made into something just gorgeous, with all the facilities, and six or seven hundred seats. In 1946 a man approached me and gave me to read a story that he wrote about his own family. The name of the book was *The Heroic Family*. He asked me if it was possible to turn the book into a play for the stage. I read it a few times. I liked it very much and I said I'll try my best. I called quite a few people to talk about it, actors, amateurs, professionals. For quite a few weeks we worked, and when we put it on it was very well received. The *Bamidbar* wrote a very good critique about it. I was so encouraged, I started looking for something else to put on. I found a beauty. A comedy by Sholom Aleichem called *Two Hundred Thousand,* about a man who wins the lottery.

Frania

I was going with Israel to all the rehearsals. Just from sitting and listening, I knew everybody's part, that was the funniest thing. When opening night came, one of the actresses got sick with a hundred and three temperature, and she couldn't come to play. Israel came running home and he said, "Malka's sick and the opening night is tonight. You have to go to play the part." I said, "Me?" He said, "Come on, you know all the lines." What could I do? I had to go play it. They said I was terrific. I don't know. I did it only for Israel. Oh, it was such a terrific success in that time, wonderful.

Israel

Later on, the culture committee called a meeting with all the three directors in Föhrenwald — Wisokodworski, Sandler, and me. We talked and talked, and agreed, and disagreed. Wisokodworski wanted to go separate, and he went with a few people. But me and Sandler, we came together and we made from our two troupes one troupe. We called it Neger. So we were two directors, and we both were acting. We got along just beautifully. The truth is Sandler did most of the directing. We put on a play *Gold Digger,* also written by Sholom Aleichem, and it came out just wonderful, we had a big success. Everybody came to see it, from all over Munich and the other camps, everybody came to see that play, it was just marvellous. Besides this, I performed some monologues, and we were travelling with the plays around the camps in Germany, and entertained the people. In that time, when we weren't performing, we went to Munich to see German theatre. The truth is, they made excellent theatre. Later on, in 1948,

Sandler and I went to a German drama school run by a very learned man, a theatre director named Heinz Galetzki, and a professor of drama. We enjoyed it very, very much and we both received diplomas.

Frania

When Israel started in the theatre, we got a lot of packages. He didn't get paid with money, but paid with products. We had so much coffee, you know, Israel bought himself a motorcycle. The coffee could buy anything. He brought it up to that big room, and he was driving around the table. When you're young, you know…I said, "If you not going to get rid of that motorcycle, honest to God, I'm leaving." I couldn't take it. In the house, in the room, he was driving around the motorcycle. I said, "After the whole war, I have to get killed by a motorcycle?" He got rid of it, I don't know what he did with it, but he got rid of it.

Israel

I bought a car, a beautiful BMW that was driven around in the war by a Gestapo. You know, when you're an actor you have to go in style. In 1948, I wanted to go to Israel already. I went to Munich to the Histadrut, the Zionist organization, to inform them that I'm ready to go. "How are you going to make a living there?" they asked me. "I'm not a beggar," I said to them. "Money I haven't got. But I have a beautiful BMW and I want to take it with me. I could drive taxi." They said, "How can you take a big car? It's not allowed." I said, "I'm a good mechanic. I'll take it apart, in pieces. I'll put it in boxes, and when I'll be in Israel, I'll put it together." They said, "That's fine. But we will take fifty-one percent of what you make from that car." I got so mad, I said, "What? I'm going to work and the car is mine, and you're going to take away my living for no reason at all?" "Take it or leave it," they said to me.

So I left. The hell with socialism! I went away with a broken heart.

Frania
We would be in Israel if this incident wouldn't happen.

Israel
They did that not only to us, you know. I don't know if that was government policy or not. I know one single thing, that people went to Australia, here to Canada, to United States, all over, and left everything, and didn't go to Israel on account of that.

Frania
We moved after a year from Illinois Street to Tennessee Avenue. Every house was the same, but now we had a little more privacy. Malkale and Chaskel Rosenblatt fell in love and left for France, where his sister was living. So it was left only me and Israel and my uncle Chaim who married a wonderful woman, Eva. The four of us shared the new place. Downstairs there were two rooms, and upstairs was one large room. Israel bought some boards and he made us beds. Oh, there I had a palace. Eva and I were good housekeepers. So when Israel got some parcels every week, we took out some coffee, gave it to the Germans and we bought paint and we painted the whole house, me and Eva. We got good mattresses, we hired a man to build a stove, and we got everything from trading coffee. Our house was always full of people, it was like a centre, you know? And the friends we made there, we still have them. It was a happy time, what can I tell you, in the middle of all the chaos of the war just finished, and not knowing what's going to happen with our future, it was probably one of the happiest times of our lives there in that displaced-persons camp.

Israel

We started looking for some good plays, something classical. We found *The Golem,* written in the twenties by H. Leivick, one of the greatest Jewish writers. That play was really with a message. First of all, it originated with a legend in Prague, Czechoslovakia. The legend was that there lived a very learned rabbi, called the Maharal, respected by all the Jews in the world, and even by non-Jewish people. That was in the sixteenth century, a time of many pogroms, killing of the Jews. The story was that a priest killed a Christian boy and accused the Jews of killing the child ritually for his blood which the priest said the Jews used to make matzo, the unleavened bread for Passover. That particular lie is old like the hills. Even recently, in Russia, Jews were accused of this. In the legend, the Maharal, to protect the Jewish population, created a man from clay, a kind of Frankenstein monster, a golem, by using the rituals of cabala, mysticism. This golem was about nine feet tall, and he was very powerful. The Maharal was forced later to destroy that golem, because he started to kill his own people. One message of the play was that you cannot use murder to fight murder because it destroys you in the end. I played the part of the golem on stilts. I was very much known in the camp and nobody could believe that it's me. We had a big success with *The Golem,* mostly because of the vision Jacob Sandler had as director. All over they were talking about it, how beautiful it was made, how beautiful we played it. When the curtains opened, we heard from the audience, "Ah!" It became so quiet, that you could drop a pin. It was just unbelievable. One night, an American army general from Munich came to see the play. He didn't understand Yiddish, but he came back after, grabbed me, and he said he saw a lot of plays in the United States, but this was an amazing experience. To prepare that production, we were reading *The Golem* quite a few weeks. And the more we were reading, the more we saw that nothing has changed. From the Inquisition in Spain, through the Holocaust, to now — nothing has changed. In that time, Frania was pregnant with you. During the first act, one night, a friend of mine came backstage, he was standing at the side and he practically yelled at me: "Israel Israel!" *Mazel tov!* You have a son!" I cried for happiness and I nearly fell off my stilts. And I had to play, the show has to go on. What can I tell you? I played the second act, like never before.

Frania
Israel was playing in the theatre and I was making a coffee cake for after the play. Suddenly the labour pains started so bad I went right down to the floor. A neighbour took me to the camp hospital, two minutes away. I tell you, they didn't have time to do nothing, I went on the table, my water broke and you swam out. You know, I was in a corner room so there were windows on two sides. When you were born, a little bird flew to one window, knocked three times with his mouth and then flew to the other window and knocked again. The nurse who was there said, "You're going to be lucky, your family."

Israel
We made a big celebration but the champagne we had prepared was stolen by some Roumanians. Soon we had to think to go somewhere, out of Europe. I wouldn't stay in Europe for no money. Chaim and Eva had papers to go to America already so we wanted to go too. At that time, there was a Jewish organization, HIAS, that was helping Jewish refugees to come to America. I went to them, in Munich, put in my name, and a man gave me an interview. He said, "You are Israel Rubinek, the grandson of the rabbi from Busko Zdroj?" I said, "Yes, how do you

know about me?" He answered, "Never mind. You are not going to America. You will go to Israel." I didn't understand why he said this and who he was and how he knew about me. And till this day I never found out. And I could not get papers to go to the United States.

Frania

My uncle Leon made arrangements, through his wife's relatives, to immigrate to Canada, and they were in Montreal already. My uncle Chaim wrote to Leon and said that Leon should sponsor us to come to Canada. Canada let you come in that time, but you had to have a close relative to sponsor you. So Chaim said to Leon, "Don't worry. I'll pay for it." Because he knew his brother Leon wouldn't give away a cent.

Israel

Nine months after you were born, in May of '49, we went on a ship, the *Scythia,* to Canada.

Frania

That was a ship? It was meant for cattle, not people. The whole boat was refugees. I was so sick on that trip, other people had to look after you. There was a sailor, I remember, he took pity on me and he was bringing me oranges to make me well.

Israel

I gave that sailor a beautiful cigarette lighter for an egg, so you could have something healthy to eat. I remember there was a Christian missionary on that ship, he came to me and wanted me to believe in Jesus. I said to him, "Why do I need the Son when I already have the Father?" We arrived in Quebec City, at the port, and people from the Jewish Congress welcomed us and also a delegation from the Canadian government. I came down from the ship and I cried. That's it. I'm alive. I'm here.

Frania

I don't know who it was, but a French-Canadian man came over to Israel, put his arm around him, and said, "Don't you worry. Don't cry. You're in a good country." And then he gave us a loaf of white sliced bread and ten dollars.

Israel

In Montreal we stayed for a few days with her uncle Leon and his wife. They made us feel very low. She would say to me, "You know, I can't even think in Yiddish any more. Only in English." That burned me up. She was a greenhorn, just like me. And she would tell me not to eat like this, not to walk like that, do this, do that — just like servants, she was treating us.

We went to live in a little room, no windows — in the daytime, it was night-time. And I was sitting there with you on my lap and thinking that before, in the camp, I was a somebody and now I was nothing. I got a job in a fur factory, sixty hours a week for thirty-six dollars.

Frania

We saved money from Germany, five hundred dollars, but we had to use it for "key money" to get an apartment. So for two dollars we bought a table and for another four dollars we had two chairs, and we slept on the floor.

Israel

And then I began to understand my new country. A man came in and said we could fill the whole apartment with furniture. Not to pay him now, just to give five dollars a week. I said to him, "You don't know me. How can you do it?" He said, "Welcome to the New Land."

Frania

Then Israel got a job in a factory as a presser. That was considered the lowest job for immigrants. But he was working only forty hours a week and making a hundred twenty dollars. People that knew us from Föhrenwald came to me and said, "What happened to your husband? He was a director, an actor. How can you let him go so low? A presser?" I said, "Look. We have a child. We're starting a new life. We take charity from nobody. He's the same man he always was. Yes, he goes into the factory as a presser. But when he comes out, for me, he's the prime minister."

Part Five

The Journey Back

In the fall of 1985 my mother told me that she had just
received a letter from Zofia Banya. Maniek was now fifty years
old and Ludwig had died a few years before. Zofia wrote that
she wanted to see my parents again before she dies.

Over the last forty years my parents had kept in touch with
the Banyas by letter. My mother had been sending them
money and parcels of clothing for years. She had been afraid to
go back — the memories might be too much to take. But this
last letter of Zofia's finally convinced her to go.

Plans were made for the trip, and naturally, I wanted to go
with them. In the winter of '86, I discussed with a friend of
mine, Vic Sarin, the possibility of shooting the journey back as
a documentary film. Vic is one of Canada's best cinematog-
raphers and I had worked with him many times.

My parents liked the idea. They knew Vic, trusted him, and
felt more comfortable going back to Poland in some kind of
official context.

Vic and I approached Kathy Smalley, a producer at the
Canadian Broadcasting Corporation, and we arranged a deal
very quickly. Vic and Kathy would co-direct the project, and I
would co-produce it with the CBC. Vic would be the cine-
matographer, and we would take with us a sound man, Ian
Challis, and one assistant, Terry Zazulek. We decided to leave
for Poland in August of '86.

That spring we worked on the scenario for the shoot and I
familiarized Vic and Kathy with the material I had collected

over the years from my parents. I wanted the preparation to be as detailed as possible because I knew that once I was in Poland, I didn't really want to be part of the film-making process; I wanted to experience the trip with my parents.

My parents arrived at my house in Toronto on August fourth. They had come from Ottawa, tired and excited. When we began to shoot some scenes of us preparing to leave, I realized that Mom was by far the best of us on camera — very spontaneous. She told me privately that Dad had not really wanted to go back, but now, in an atmosphere of lights, camera and "action," he was very excited about it.

We arrived in Warsaw on August seventh. The crew headed for the hotel, but my parents and I were met by a Polish couple, Teresa and Alex. Mom had met Teresa in Ottawa a couple of years before and had been nice to her, and now the favour was being returned. While driving us to the hotel, Teresa and Alex spoke to my parents in Polish, which was translated to me in Yiddish and soon there was English, Polish and Yiddish indiscriminately thrown around in the car. In the confusion and excitement, my parents asked about the creation of the Warsaw Ghetto Monument, which was immediately misinterpreted as a request to go there before going to the hotel. Suddenly there we were at the monument to pay our respects. We were tired and unprepared — yet it was all familiar, as if we'd been paying respect for years.

Later, at the hotel Dad looked through the Warsaw telephone book and found a "Rubinek." (He does that wherever he goes in the world.) He called them but the woman who answered said she was not family, not Jewish. Dad was very suspicious.

Meanwhile Mom went to visit an old friend, Anka Rapoport. When she came back, she was quite shaken. In the old days in Pinczow Anka had been a sophisticated, elegant, rich woman. Now she was eighty-three years old and living in poverty. Mom promised Anka she would take me and Dad to see her the next

ïa Banya in 1986, the day of the reunion.

Ludwig and Zofia's old farmhouse in which Frania and Israel hid during the war.

Israel looking around inside the old farmhouse.

Maniek and Israel during the reunion.

Zofia, Israel and Frania outside the new house in which Zofia and
Maniek now live.

Israel in Lodz, standing by the wall where people were lined up and shot for breaking the curfew.

The ruins of Frania's family home on the square in Pinczow.

Israel at the entrance of his apartment house in Lodz, where he saw his father for the last time.

Izzel and Moniek during the reunion

with his mother and father in Pinczow. Israel and Frania used to rendezvous here when they were
ng.

day. We also planned to see Shmulek Finer, who had been one of my dad's closest friends before the war. They hadn't seen each other since that day in 1942 when the Jews in Pinczow were deported.

After dinner, I spoke to Kathy about feelings that were awakening in me: the need to rid myself of Dad's images of the war (as if *I* had lived it); to understand my reactions to his bitterness — feelings that have somehow been passed on to me.

The crew had gone on ahead to set up at Shmulek's place so that they could capture his meeting with my parents.

Teresa's son-in-law Jacek picked us up at the hotel and we arrived at a park near Shmulek's apartment. On a signal from Kathy we drove into the lane of the apartment building. Shmulek and his wife, Ziuta, were waiting for us.

The reunion was instantly very emotional. I didn't know whether it was the fact that they'd changed so much that affected them so deeply, but all of them were speechless. Nobody noticed the camera running.

Shmulek could barely walk; two of us had to help him get up and sit down. I found out later that he could, in fact, get around quite well, but he was overcome by emotion. His wife said that he had spent the previous day in tears.

I discovered that Shmulek's son lived in New York. Two years ago he was in Montreal visiting friends and happened to see one of my TV shows. When the credits came on, he recognized the name Rubinek because his father had spoken of the old days and my dad's name had come up a lot. Shmulek hadn't known that my parents were alive and my parents had assumed Shmulek was dead.

The Finers had been living as non-Jews for forty years. Ziuta told me she didn't want her children to grow up with bitterness and so they never dwelt on the past. When she said that I looked at my dad; he looked away. Although we were talking in Yiddish (the only language common to all of us), we had to pretend we were speaking German so that the Polish maid, who had been with them for twenty years, would not suspect we were Jews. Ziuta told me that after the war, many Jews with vengeance in their hearts became members of the Communist Party, and that helped provoke new anti-Semitism.

I began to realize there were quite a few Jews living in Poland today, hiding their roots. Officially there are five thousand Jews left in all of Poland. Before the war, ten percent of the population was Jewish. In the big cities, like Warsaw and Lodz, it was as much as forty percent. Now the entire country has about as many Jews as used to live in Pinczow.

Shmulek and my parents were awed by each other's survival and the changes that the years had brought. Slowly they began to recognize in each other the faces of the friends they had last seen in their early twenties.

Then the war stories started.

It was raining and we couldn't get a cab out of Shmulek's place. We had promised my mom's friend Anka Rapoport that we would visit her. Ziuta found a stranger willing to drive us in his private car — for a price. She said, "Just give him an American dollar, and he'll be happy."

The man drove us back into Warsaw from the suburbs. When we got to the little street where Anka lived, I gave the guy a dollar and also a couple of hundred zlotys. I made the mistake of handing it to him in an obvious way. He grabbed the money and quickly hid it below the dashboard. I then remembered that giving people American money was illegal. The man was very frightened. I was surprised how nervous he was.

We walked into a courtyard where there were children playing. They watched us very closely because, I guess, we were dressed differently from other people. There was a little boy, maybe six years old, who had shown my mother where Anka lived when she came the previous day. Mom gave him a candy and he took us to Anka's room.

I don't know how long she'd been waiting for us. Shmulek had kept us longer than we'd planned. I was nervous about going in — I was afraid that everything might be depressing. But Anka's room was airy and looked very neat. She had put on a nice dress, and I could see right away that she was still a very beautiful woman. She had the most incredibly exquisite bone structure. She was blind in one eye. Mom said she was always like that — they used to call her "one-eyed Anka." None of that mattered: she was lovely and elegant. Anka was very happy to see us. My parents had sent the whole world pictures of me, of course, and notices of how I was doing in my acting career. So Anka had received various newspaper clippings and knew all about me.

She lived in one room. We all sat and I begged everyone to speak Yiddish so I could follow the conversation. The old lady couldn't remember much Yiddish, and my parents, as usual, lapsed back into Polish, but somehow I found I was beginning to pick up more and more of what was being said.

Whenever a painful subject arose, mom and dad would warn each other to steer clear. They had seen how Shmulek couldn't really take it, and Anka was older and frailer. It became clear to me that my parents, unlike the people we were visiting, seemed to be able to talk about the past. Anka's friend Helena from next door came in. She was probably in her eighties, a short squat woman with almost no hair, with thick painted-on eyebrows and very red lipstick. She spoke English quite well and explained that she had worked in England during the war. She added proudly that she spoke French, German and Yiddish, too. Since the war Helena and Anka had hidden their Jewishness. Anka and Helena lived in poverty but when tea was served, it was done with formality and grace. The cake arrived on a lovely plate. Anka even insisted that Helena give us tiny silver forks with which to eat our cake.

When Helena left, my parents and Anka started to speak about the old days. Anka used to buy her clothes in Paris. She had been one of the richest women in Pinczow. My mom said that when Anka walked down the street, the cobblestones trembled.

When it was time to leave, Anka said, "I'll never see you again." She said it very simply, with a little smile.

Before coming we had tried to figure out what kind of present to give her. At Shmulek's my mother had wondered out loud if she should take anything at all; she remembered Anka as a very proud woman. Ziuta had said, "The best thing is to give her some money and she'll give it to her friend, and they'll buy whatever they want." Now we decided that my mother should give her some money — privately. I went outside to wait for Jacek who was picking us up. When he arrived I started to go back in but Dad said, "Not now. She's giving her the money."

I waited for a while and then knocked.

My mother replied, "Not yet, not yet."

Finally Mom came out and we said goodbye to Anka. I asked Mom, "Well? Did she take the money?"

Mom said, "Are you kidding? Absolutely not."

And my father said, "I told you so."

It was the usual way things went.

Mom said Anka was too proud to take it but we'd buy her a nice blouse, that's what she'd like. The next day my mother went out shopping and found a beautiful silk blouse for Anka.

I'm going through a strange feeling of experiencing Poland and the political climate of the place, the people, at the same time as I'm on a very personal journey. My mother seems almost completely oblivious to the politics, except that she just wants to come home to Canada and kiss the ground and thank God she doesn't have to live this way. My father's attitude is fairly fixed: the totalitarian system is to blame and he hates Communism even more. As for me, I don't really know much. I'm told that farmers are doing better than they ever did before, but people seem to have a rough time just living day to day. The west has spoiled me, for sure.

You know what? I feel more like a "Jew" here than I did back home. And what the hell is a Jew anyway? For sure my blood is all mixed up, like the rest of the universe. And Polish blood runs in me too, I can bet on it. So these are my people too, and I want to know what's going on with them. I didn't expect to be as interested as I am. I guess I'm getting an inkling of what it must have been like for those Polish Jews in the thirties who were just beginning to break away from ghetto life and become interested in the world around them — only to be cut down by their neighbours in their hour of need.

The added paradox here is that it seems that the Poles' salvation, what could help release them from Russia's yoke, is the Catholic church. The same church that was the cause of so much of my forefathers' misery.

August the ninth was the day we set off for Pinczow and everybody was very excited. We knew it was going to be a big day emotionally, and so we didn't talk about it too much.

Teresa had gotten up early that morning to buy fruit at the market for our journey. Mom, Dad and I were to travel together in one car. The rest of the crew was going on ahead to set up.

My mother told me she had given a dollar bill to the cleaning lady who did our rooms at the hotel and was shocked when the woman fell on her knees and kissed my mother's hands. Mom was so embarrassed, she said, "Get up! Get up! What are you doing?" She had to promise the cleaning lady that if we came back, we'd try to get these same rooms.

The trip out was our first into the Polish countryside. The names of many towns had a familiar ring to them, especially the ones my father recognized: where there used to be a famous rabbi, or where a member of the family once lived, or where he had visited when young. We passed a town called Konskie, the birthplace of the first Rubinek who came to Pinczow, according to my father.

We arrived in Pinczow and drove around that square I'd

heard so much about. Everything had changed. The park in the middle of the square had been totally rebuilt; all the houses were different. Dad said the town seemed five or six times bigger than he remembered it. My great-grandfather's flour mill used to be on the outskirts and now was quite central. It was very hard for them to recognize landmarks, but the church at the end of the square was the same. The house where Dad used to live with his aunt Hadas, the house that was attached to the church, had been destroyed.

We took one drive around and then went to the hostel where the crew was staying. The director of the hostel, Mr Glut, had an apartment for me and my parents, on the outskirts of town, on the road to Busko Zdroj.

It was amazing for me to finally be there.

My parents were in a state of shock — sometimes as excited as kids on a field trip, sometimes in a trance, unnaturally quiet and introspective.

At five o'clock a marriage was to take place at the church and Vic wanted to shoot a typical Polish wedding, so we all went to see the bride and groom as they came out. While we were standing outside the church my dad wandered over to a spot in the middle of the street. He was standing on the place where his home once was. A man walked over to him and tapped him on the shoulder and said, "Is your name Rubinek?" The man was the son of the barber that used to be my mother's neighbour on the square. After a little while, some other people joined us and they started talking about who was alive and who wasn't.

Then something extraordinary happened. One of the Polish women said to my parents, "So you see, not all of you were killed. There's some of you left." My mother reacted strongly, saying, "What are you talking about? Is there one Jew left in Pinczow? You're talking like a child. I may be alive but millions are not."

I guess Mom must have caught something in this woman's tone that pushed a button. Later my mother said she realized that all she was doing was venting steam and looking for, as she put it, "a loophole."

Word of our presence travelled like wildfire, and the cars we were driving, white Ford Tauruses, made us very conspicuous.

Two people joined our crew: Stan Baran, husband of the cultural attaché at the Canadian Embassy in Warsaw and Eva Stanek. Stan was our locations manager, and Eva was the liaison to Interpress, the official government media agency that had granted us permission to do the documentary. Officially, Eva was our translator, but what she really did was report our daily activities to the government. She admitted all this quite freely.

Eva, who was about thirty and studiously intellectual, had worked with Claude Lantzmann as a translator when he filmed *Shoah,* which is the Hebrew word for holocaust. *Shoah* is a nine hour documentary about the bureaucracy of genocide. Eva was very sympathetic to our project and felt that we would show the Polish people in a light more positive than *Shoah* had. Well, in this case, the positive was inevitable because central to our story was the fact that Polish farmers had saved Jewish lives. We did, however, intend to balance the documentary with a few stories that were not so pleasant, and I wondered how Eva would react.

I spoke to Eva about my father's bitterness towards the Poles. "Why?" she wondered. So I told her, for example, how the Poles pointed out Jewish houses to the Germans on the day that Pinczow's Jews were deported to the concentration camps and how the image had burned itself into my father's eyes. I also tried to explain that for me this trip was an attempt to divest myself of the bitterness which I somehow had come to share. She seemed to understand.

On the way back to the apartment, I happened to be with Eva in the car as we passed by the old flour mill.

I said, "You know, after the war, in 1945, the Polish partisans tried to kill my parents at that mill."

She said, "Are you sure?"

"Look," I said. "There was an infamous pogrom in Kielce where Jews were murdered after the war."

She said, "Oh well, everyone knows about that."

"Well, why is it so hard for you to believe it happened here too, forty kilometres away?"

"But why?"

And so I told her a famous joke. A little old Jewish man is chased by the Nazis. They catch him and put him up against a wall and say, "Tell us, Jew, who started the war? Well, the little old Jew is no fool. "The Jews," he says. "And the bicycle riders." The Nazis look at him and say, "Why the bicycle riders?" And the little old man replies, "Why the Jews?"

On the morning of August twelfth we went down to the square and saw what used to be my mother's house. All the houses on the square had been rebuilt since the fire in 1939, all the houses except, amazingly, my mother's house. The front of the house was still a burnt-out shell, the back had been rebuilt by my mother's family in 1940.

My mother spent the morning in front of the camera talking about the burning of the square and the shooting in the churchyard. As soon as she started to tell the story, she began to relive it. I wondered whether it was right to put her through the trauma, but the fact was my parents needed to share what had happened to them. It was almost as if the act of sharing their history validated the experience. The film allowed my parents to put their thoughts and feelings into a context and gave them courage to let their feelings go.

As we were filming, a woman approached the crew and asked to meet my mother. She was a Polish lady who had gone to school with Mom. We wanted to catch this reunion on film, so we made the arrangements without telling my mother what was going on. We simply arrived at the apartment building where the Polish lady lived, and placed my mother on the sidewalk about twenty yards away from the entrance to the building. We started shooting and then called out to the Polish lady. She came out of her doorway, glanced at my mother and stopped. She couldn't move. Slowly at first, they approached each other. My mother was a bit confused. It took a few seconds for her to recognize her old friend. Then, completely oblivious to the camera, they wept and embraced each other.

We went inside the Polish lady's apartment and she showed us old school pictures that she had kept. Seeing my mother as a child in a class of Jewish and non-Jewish children, I got a sense of a whole culture that I was somehow a part of and yet knew next to nothing about. There was Mom at nine, at thirteen, at seventeen. I started to break down when I saw those photographs, I was so moved.

Later in the day we had to return to the apartment because my mother had forgotten her glasses. The lady's son was there, a man in his twenties. They started to talk and eventually came round to what happened to the Jews in the war. My parents didn't force the subject, but the young man was eager to hear them talk about it. My mother said, "Listen, if I would have gone to your mother, my school friend, and asked her to hide me and my family, what could she say? She would say that she's terrified for her own family's survival. That I could understand. But it was those Poles who knew where the Jews were hiding and then pointed them out to the Nazis, that I don't know how to forgive." And the young man started to cry and said, "I understand, I understand."

Why do I keep wishing I could go through these experiences with my parents, as they actually went through them? Why is it that I identify so strongly with their history and why do I have this eagerness to relive it? Why do I have these dreams, not quite nightmares, that I could suddenly — like the twilight zone — snap

*my fingers and bam! I'll be there and know exactly what happened,
be able to watch them go through it, and find myself go through it
as well? It seems to be deeper than trying to understand the
Holocaust or even who my parents are. I feel as though I'm
searching through the rubble for recognizable human artefacts and
finding them in the oddest place, my own heart. It must be obvious
to whoever's listening that this is called "looking for roots." These
are my people, this is where they come from, this is where they
lived, died, suffered, had joy. This is my homeland. I don't know
how I'll feel if I go to Israel, but I'm sure it won't be like this. It isn't
a happy feeling, but it's real. I have a sense that it's affecting me in
ways that I will only understand in years to come.*

The reunion with the Banyas was set for Sunday, August tenth.
We had been kept apart for quite a long time because Vic had
to film the Banyas getting ready for us on the farm. Eventually
we drove out to them near the little village of Wlochy. I'd been
hearing stories for years and years and suddenly I had a geo-
graphical reality that fixed them in my mind. I had imagined a
kind of fairy tale country, made up of millions of images from
movies and television, stories and books. And all these images
got mixed up: trees and hills changed places — the sky, the
buildings, the people themselves wandered around in my
imagination with no connection to each other. Now it was all
real. I felt I could have been born there.

We drove into the farm, all nervous, very tense. My mother
had terrible stomach cramps, but thank God, she didn't have
one of her migraines. She said, "Well, listen, I can't cry any
more so all my feelings go to my stomach and twist it in a
knot." My father was playing it very cool, saying, "If they start
to ask for money right away, I'm not sure how I'm going to
react. If they're cool, I'm going to be cool." Well, when we got
through that gate, there was a semi-circle of grandchildren,
sons-in-law, daughters — I didn't know who was who — and in
the middle of it, on a bench was a tiny old lady in a babushka,

Zofia. And there was Maniek, who looked nothing like I expected; he looked as old as my father. In fact, they looked alike. My father went running up to him, all cool gone. My mother ran to Zofia, and they all kept trading hugs and kisses and touching each other as if they couldn't believe it was real. I just stood there and watched and cried.

We stayed till nine that night talking, laughing, crying. It was simply a very, very happy day.

The next day we went up to the little hill overlooking Pinczow where my mother and father used to walk, and I guess, neck when they were young. We filmed my parents in front of a church monument, a huge block of stone with inscriptions carved into it by lovers dating back to 1689. Seeing the two of them on that spot transformed them in my eyes to the young lovers they once were. It was indescribably beautiful. I felt privileged, blessed, to see my parents in a way that most children never do. There was a break in the filming and my parents were sitting, holding hands. I was about twenty yards away, just watching them. They looked at me with tenderness and love and were quietly talking to each other about how nice I looked. They didn't know that I could overhear them, that the wind was blowing their words my way. It was a stunning moment. I felt a hundred and fifty years old and five years old at the same time. It was a magic place. It had been raining all day, but when we got to the hill the sun came out. They seem to bring miracles on themselves, my mother and father. They're quite a team.

"Yiskor" is a Hebrew word that means "remember." It probably dates back in our culture to the destruction of Solomon's Temple. It's a kind of unwritten commandment, an admonition to children, and to the children's children to remember the history of their people. Remember the suffering. Remember so that it won't happen again. Somehow, along with that edict to remember, a sea of hatred, bitterness is passed on. My mother and my father gave me *not only the ammunition to deal with the past but also their own dark feelings, and I have had trouble taking one apart from the other. I guess whether you're talking about Catholics or Protestants, or Israelis and Arabs, or Germans or Poles, wherever you go in the world, some father is passing on to some son the seeds of blood. I've seen so much courage and so much love while I've been here that, for me, the knot is untying, the paradox is unravelling. When I was younger, it was an intellectual conceit to be humanistic — we're all brothers, I'm not a Jew, I'm not a Canadian, I'm not a Pole, not this, not that. Now I feel that it's not until I understand specifically who I am, where I come from, that I can begin to understand how I relate to the rest of the human race. And that feeling of brotherhood is finally well deserved from my head to my heart.*

Epilogue

A Word About My Method

This book is the result of ten years of interviews with my mother and father. That's a long time and I didn't plan it that way. During this period I was living in New York and Toronto while my parents were either in Ottawa or Miami. My career as an actor placed its own demands on my time and so, I would say, I spent an average of six to eight weeks a year on the interview part of the work. The rest of the time was spent transcribing the material and then removing my voice from it. I was left with a series of monologues and occasional dialogue that had to be put into chronological order.

I took out my own voice because it got in the way of the story. I suppose that my probing, cajoling and arguments have some value, but then the book would have been about the three of us and I wanted it to be about them. The truth is, I am there, on every page; it's me they're talking to.

Most of the time I interviewed my parents separately, but occasionally when I felt the topic warranted it, I had them both in the same room. The finished work shows this quite clearly.

One more thing: my parents speak English with a strong Polish-Yiddish accent and that is reflected in the way they put sentences together. I've tried to be true to the grammar and syntax of their voices. Listening to them, however, and reading their words are different experiences, and sometimes their thoughts and feelings, so clear on tape, seemed muddled and opaque on the page. When grammatical mistakes resulted in confusion, I had to "clean it up" slightly.

The fact that the work spanned so many years allowed me to refine my technique as an interviewer. Once I had decided on the period I wanted to work with — 1936 to 1948, the year they met to the year I was born — and once their basic story was down on tape, I had the opportunity to probe their feelings along with the facts.

I was persistent and they were open-hearted. More than anything else, that's what made this book happen.